D1231354

Virginia Road Biking

Accurate Maps, Cue Sheets

& Elevation Profiles

Detailed Directions • Beautiful Scenery

To Julie & Fred,
Alice & I hope you'll get to
Virginia & enjoy some of the rides in
the book!

KEVIN WATSON

On your left!

ALICE MUELLERWEISS

Kevin

FOREL PUBLISHING COMPANY, LLC

Published by the Forel Publishing Company, LLC
3999 Peregrine Ridge Ct., Woodbridge, VA 22192

Printed by Commercial Press, Inc., Stephens City, Virginia

Published in the United States of America

EAN: 978-1-60371-190-6
ISBN: 1-60371-190-2

What others are saying about this book:

Andy Clarke

"Whether you are new to the area or have thousands of miles under your belt, this guidebook has that one essential ingredient everyone is looking for: the inside scoop on where to ride. You know the authors have ridden every mile themselves as you read their descriptions, follow the turns, and trace the route information. I can't wait to get out and ride them myself!" - **Andy Clarke, President, *League of American Bicyclists***

Joan Bricker on the road in Cuba

"I became fast friends with Alice and Kevin during a road bike adventure across Italy a few years ago. I regularly go on several cycling vacations each year in North America and Europe, and thoroughly enjoy visiting Virginia to ride with Kevin and Alice whenever possible. I really appreciated the route notes they prepared for me because they are so thorough and focus on scenic areas with low-traffic, interesting rest-stops, wineries, and of course the beautiful Virginia countryside. The selection of routes appeal to every type of ride and ability level. The routes depicted in this book are some of my favorites that you too will no doubt enjoy." - **Joan Bricker, Avid Cyclist, Calgary, Alberta, Canada**

Ed Cosgrove giving a route talk prior
to a Team in Training training ride

"Kevin and Alice have supported the Leukemia and Lymphoma Society's Team in Training since 2005. By donating all of their profit from this fun, informative book, they are continuing their fight against blood cancers. GO TEAM!" - **Ed Cosgrove, Cycling Coach, National Capital Area Team in Training**

Rich and Maureen Wierman, left, enjoying a Carolina Tailwinds Happy
Hour with fellow Carolina Tailwinds customer, John Mayer

"Thank you, Kevin & Alice for putting into one book some of the most enjoyable rides Northern Virginia has to offer. You have obviously done your homework! We look forward to many more miles with you in the beautiful Virginia countryside!" -- **Rich & Maureen Wierman, Cyclists & Carolina Tailwinds Customers**

Contents

About the Authors

Alice and Kevin in Urbino, Italy

We are road biking enthusiasts living in Northern Virginia. We enjoy feeling the warm (and cooling) breezes and seeing the beautiful views that road biking brings. We are both Army veterans; currently, Alice works at the Department of Veterans Affairs, while Kevin works for Department of the Army. In Kevin's spare time, he is a tour guide for Carolina Tailwinds Bicycling Vacations.

We began road biking about ten years ago and were drawn out of the D.C. metro area to find wider and less congested roads. Exploration led us to create some beautiful rides, meet terrific people and make new friends, and eat some delicious food! We have ridden our bikes throughout the mid-Atlantic, California, Nevada, Colorado, Texas, Germany, Italy, and the Caribbean.

Combining our love for cycling with our determination to help cure blood cancer we are donating the profits of this book to the Leukemia and Lymphoma Society (LLS). When our son, Jason was diagnosed with Hodgkin's Lymphoma in 2004 we were grateful to the society for the knowledge and support provided to cancer patients and families. We participated in a Team in Training (TNT) event, cycling the beautiful Lake Tahoe and were overwhelmed by similar stories. When the last few miles of Alice's first century ride became tough, she was able to spin through knowing the fight her son was experiencing was much more challenging. Shortly after our son finished his treatment, Alice's father, John was diagnosed with Non-Hodgkin's Lymphoma (Mantle B-Cell). Our son, Jason is in remission, is married to the former Lindsey Elam and has a darling son, Owen. Alice's father, John lost his fight after a three year battle.

Jason and Lindsey with grandson, Owen - TNT not only saves lives but also enables more lives!

Cycling brings new adventures at every turn and interesting and rewarding opportunities. We wish you all great fun, safe rides, and lasting memories of beautiful Virginia!

Preface – Note to the Reader

This is an exciting time to be a road biking enthusiast. Road biking, especially from the Washington, D.C. metro area and throughout northern Virginia continues to change - for the better.

There is not enough room in one book to include everything you would like to know about road biking in northern Virginia and the northern Shenandoah Valley. Consequently, we have provided a listing of cycling clubs and cycling shops in northern Virginia, as well as après-cycling attractions and activities.

Kevin Watson and Alice Muellerweiss
Alexandria, Virginia

Acknowledgements

We have not attempted to cite in the text all the authorities and sources consulted in the preparation of this book. To do so would require more space than is available. The list would include state and local governments, libraries, periodicals, websites and many individuals.

Information and illustrations have been contributed to this book by David LeBlanc, Bob Marsh, Carol Gardner, Ronald Montgomery, Curt Southern, Bruce Kramme, Dan Poynter, Ed Cosgrove, Bill Edelblut, Steve Mitchell, Al Williams, Joan Bricker, Michael Fuqua, Rich and Maureen Wierman, Ken Rose, Dr. Harry Dinella, Hank Henry, Andy Kirkner, and many others...

Special thanks go to everyone at Commercial Press in Stephens City for their patience, technical assistance, enthusiasm, and friendship. Karen (Suzi) White is awesome! Not only are Bill and Sue Grim our printers, they are our friends. They truly made this book happen.

We sincerely thank all these fine people. We hope they are proud of their contribution to road biking in northern Virginia and the northern Shenandoah Valley.

Bob Marsh and Carol Gardner,
who have helped us learn the joys of road biking.

Warning – Disclaimer

This book was written to provide information to cyclists interested in road biking in northern Virginia and the northern Shenandoah Valley. It is sold with the understanding that the printer and authors are not engaged in rendering legal or other professional services pertaining to the laws and regulations of bicycling. If legal or other expert assistance is required, the services of a competent professional should be sought.

It is not the purpose of this book to reprint all the information that is otherwise available to bicycle enthusiasts, but instead to complement, amplify and supplement other information available. You are urged to read all the available material, learn as much as possible about road biking in Virginia and tailor the information to your individual needs.

Every effort has been made to make this book as complete and accurate as possible. However, *there may be mistakes*, both in typographical and in content. Additionally, due to on-going development of the Virginia road network, the specific mileage and turns on the cue sheets in this book *may require adjustments*. Therefore, this book should be should be used only as a guide which is generally current up to the printing date.

The purpose of this book is to educate and entertain. The authors and publisher shall have neither liability nor responsibility to any person or entity with respect to any loss or damage caused, or alleged to have been caused, directly or indirectly, by the information contained in this book.

If you do not wish to be bound by the above, you may return this book to the authors for a full refund.

1

Introduction

Virginia Byways sign

Virginia's varied terrain makes road biking enjoyable throughout the Commonwealth but northern Virginia and the northern portion of the Shenandoah Valley are especially rewarding places to ride. Cyclists looking for scenic rides along less traveled secondary roads - normally those numbered 600 and over - can take advantage of the Virginia Byways system. There are over 2,700 miles of Virginia Byways so designated for their scenic, cultural, historical, or recreational value. Though the rides described in this book travel predominantly on secondary roads and on several of the Virginia Byways roads, they are not centered on the Virginia Byways. Since each route described in this book shares the road with motor vehicles without special provisions for cyclists, riders must use caution on each of the routes. Many of these scenic routes have narrow pavement, and curves and hills with limited sight distances. Safety is not guaranteed on any of the routes and is the responsibility of the individual cyclist. In this book, we have made every effort to educate cyclists following our routes. Individual and group vigilance while riding will ensure not only a thoroughly enjoyable ride through the countryside but also a SAFE ride!

In the interest of full disclosure we wanted to describe our respective riding capabilities to help you gauge each route when selecting the ride you want to take. Based on the Potomac Pedalers Touring Club (PPTC) ride classification guide Alice is a CC-level rider. She averages about 10-12 mph on hills; 12-14 mph on moderate & 14-16 mph on flats. She normally averages around 13 mph on our rides in the Shenandoah Valley. Kevin is a BB-level rider. He averages about 14-16 mph on hills; 16-18 mph on moderate & 18-20 mph on flats. He normally averages around 17 mph on rides in the Shenandoah Valley.

We list the rides we present in this book from nearest to furthest from Metro D.C. However, we did not tailor the routes to the distance from Metro D.C. For instance, the Bridgewater rides are not only the furthest distance from Metro D.C., they are also two of the longer and more challenging rides in the book. They are also two of the most scenic rides and are well worth the drive to get to them. We logically organized each ride chapter by telling how to get there followed by the general lay of the land and ride description. Except for the Winchester Loop and Harrisonburg Loop rides, the route map and cue sheet pages for each ride are back-to-back on detachable paper to make it easier for you to detach the map and cue sheet and copy them prior to your ride. The cue sheets for the Winchester and Harrisonburg rides are each two pages long. The Winchester ride also has two maps and a two-page cue sheet so the maps are back-to-back and the cue sheet pages are back-to-back. The Harrisonburg chapter has the elevation profile page back-to-back with the map page and then the two cue sheet back-to-back. Finally, we end each chapter with local information on places to eat, location of bike shops - if any - and other local attractions that we hope will contribute to your enjoyment of seeing Virginia by bike.

Safe Riding

Cyclists have both a personal and community responsibility to ride safely. We all ride for enjoyment and safe riding makes for enjoyable riding. Additionally all cyclists have an inherent interest in fostering positive relations with others we encounter on the roadways - both vehicle and pedestrians. Frankly, who amongst us has not been startled by a passing cyclist - who did not warn us of their approach - while walking down a road or trail? Who has not witnessed a cyclist illegally riding on the wrong side of the road? If we all act as goodwill ambassadors to others on the roadways, we will make our collective rides more enjoyable for all.

Remember - in a collision between a bike and any motorized vehicle - YOU lose! Stay alert using all of your senses as you look ahead to see what is coming up. Listen for the sounds of engines, brakes being applied, wind rustling through the trees, loud music, the dog on the porch, the driver turning right at a stop sign but not stopping. Pick routes with bail-out options, roads with shoulders are preferable but maybe the roadway for a great ride is narrow and twisty - then pick the time of day or of the week when there's less traffic. Make your intentions known by signaling early, often and demonstratively! Use your voice rather than your horn. A loud - "Hey!!" works wonders; follow it up with a wave and smile to deflect any potential anger at getting yelled at. Practice keeping a straight line while turning to glance over your left shoulder to look for traffic coming behind you. Announce your presence to pedestrians or cyclists ahead of you by speaking up from behind (On your Left!) - don't wait and speak when you are on top of them - that is guaranteed to startle them and do one of two things - either spook them into your pathway or make them mad. Also - a basic tenet of riding should be to keep your thumbs wrapped under your handlebar - especially on an unfamiliar or shaded route. You can quickly get tossed by an unexpected bump that jerks your hands off the handlebar. Keep your **I**n **C**ase of **E**mergency (I.C.E.) information updated. Include your emergency contact person's name, phone and email; your next of kin information; blood type, allergies and insurance information.

Virginia's cycling rules are similar to most other states. Ride to the right single file and clearly signal your intentions to stop or turn. Some jurisdictions *require* the wearing of helmets but we all know to wear a helmet each time we saddle up! If riding between sunset and sunrise your bike must have a white light on its front with the light being visible at least 500 feet to the front. The bicycle must have a red reflector on the rear visible at least 600 feet to the rear. Bikes ridden on highways must have brakes that skid the wheels on dry, level, clean pavement. Bikes cannot be ridden on Interstate highways or on other controlled access highways.

Here are a few final Tips for Safe Bicycling reminders from the VDOT Bicycle Program website for safe cycling:

- Be a responsible bicyclist - obey all traffic control devices and use proper hand signals.

- Always ride with the flow of traffic.

- Dress safely - wear a helmet, wear bright colored clothing, and secure loose pant legs.

- Ride defensively - anticipate the actions of other road users and watch for road hazards.

- Pass vehicles with extreme care - turning vehicles may not see you.

- Be aware of motor vehicle blind spots whether while riding or when stopped at an intersection.

- Maximize your visibility at night - wear reflective clothing and apply reflective tape to your bicycle.

- Walk your bicycle when you get into traffic situations beyond your cycling abilities.

- Exercise great caution when riding in bus traffic - watch out for buses pulling to and from curbs and passengers getting on and off buses.

- Park your bicycle so you do not block sidewalks, handicap and building accesses, or emergency drives.

- Lock your bicycle - secure both wheels and the frame to a stationary object using a sturdy lock.

- Register or license your bicycle if required or provided by your community.

The Bike Lane, a local bike shop with locations in Burke and Reston, VA has some excellent all-around cycling tips on their website (www.thebikelane.com). Here are their safety tips for getting through intersections:

Todd Mader, owner of The Bike Lane.
Customer satisfaction is his goal.

1. Always leave yourself an out. Scan the situation and make sure you have a safe exit route in the event something crazy happens. If you can swerve into a driveway or you have left plenty of room to brake, you will drastically reduce the chances of an accident.

2. Be non-confrontational. Drivers are under a lot of stress and they can lose it at times. You might be tempted to reciprocate. However, do not because it serves no purpose and may exacerbate the situation. Instead, take a deep breath and let it go. Do not let someone else's stress rub off on you.

3. Remember to signal early. If you intend to turn at an intersection, especially if you are moving into the left-turn lane, signal early. Moreover, do not move left until it is safe to do so. If you get trapped on the right curb due to heavy traffic, wait until it is safe to get in the left-turn lane. Sometimes, it possible to turn right (if that road is less busy), execute a legal U-turn and use the light to proceed through the intersection the way you want to go.

4. Be careful not to stop on an oil slick. Motor vehicles leak oil, and the deposits are usually in the middle of the lane at an intersection. Riding through this stuff is bad for your tires and can lead to loss of traction and a crash when you start pedaling again.

5. Don't get doored! If you are approaching an intersection and parked cars are on your right, remain alert for drivers exiting their cars. Should they swing open their door, you will have to react quickly to avoid a serious crash.

6. Eye contact is key. For safety in traffic, always try to establish eye contact before moving in front of cars. When you are behind a slow-moving vehicle, try to meet the driver's eyes by looking in his mirrors and do not pass until he lets you know it is safe to.

7. Always expect the worst and ride accordingly. If you can adopt this attitude at all times, you will be safest in traffic and elsewhere.

One final thought - when cycling in traffic discretion is ALWAYS preferred to valor. Being in the legal right does not help you if a vehicle hits you and you wind up in the hospital or worse!

National Parks Fees/Passes

Two rides described within this book take you onto National Park Service lands - Prince William Forest Park and Skyline Drive within the Shenandoah National Park. For private vehicles, there are three different entry fee options from which to choose. The individual daily fee (normally $3-8) is valid for the day of purchase and the next six days. The vehicle daily fee (normally $5-$15.00) for private, non-commercial vehicles is valid for day of purchase and next six days and includes passenger cars, pickup trucks, RVs, vans, and converted buses. Finally, you may choose to purchase an Annual Interagency Pass for $80. The annual pass is valid for one full year from the first use in a Park. The Annual Interagency Pass is available online at www.store.usgs.gov/pass. If you have documented proof of permanent disability, you may request a free Access Pass, which allows entry into all public lands across the country that currently charge entrance or standard amenity fees. Obviously, your biking or traveling plans will dictate your choice but we have found the Annual Interagency Pass to be the best value for us as we easily recoup its cost with our many visits to ride in National Park Service lands in northern Virginia (Prince William Forest Park, C&O Canal, and Skyline Drive).

There is normally a Park Ranger shed at the entrance to the Park where you must stop and pay a Ranger your entry fee per vehicle or show them your annual pass. The Ranger will offer you a Park map if you want one. We highly recommend obtaining a map for your first visit to any of the Parks as they provide details for location restrooms and food/drink. The Ranger will give you a receipt and ask you to tape it to your windshield when parking so the Rangers know you have paid. When riding on Skyline Drive we normally drive up to the entrance, show the Ranger our Annual Interagency Pass and explain that we are parking at the parking area before the entrance and riding our bikes up. The Rangers have always allowed us to ride through without charging us separate fees for our two bikes.

Clothing, Tools, Food & Drink

Before getting out and riding, a quick word on clothing, tools, food and drink. Your local bike shop can outfit you cycling gear that will increase your safety while simultaneously increase your riding enjoyment. Biking shorts (or bibs and long pants for cold weather) prevent chafing and reduce saddle soreness. Bike jerseys are available in bright colors that increase your visibility to motorists. They are made of material that wicks moisture away from your body to keep you dry. Most jerseys have two - three large pockets in the back to carry tools, food and money, etc. Padded gloves help prevent numbness on longer rides and protect your hands when you fall. Speaking of falling, all experienced cyclists know it is a question of **when** you will fall, not **if** you will fall.

Speaking of tools, do not start a ride without the minimal tools to repair a flat - a patch kit or extra tube, tire levers and a pump. A multi-tool is a good investment and easily fits into a jersey pocket or a saddlebag. Most bike shops offer basic maintenance classes that minimally teach you how to adjust cables, patch a tube/tire, or replace a tube. We are members of the League of American Bicyclists and attended a basic maintenance course taught by a League Certified Instructor. Go to www.bikeleague.org for more information.

Jersey pockets can hold quite a bit of tools and/or food. Ensure your bike has two water cages and fill your water bottles before each

Kevin passing tire levers to Bill Walczak
as Bill repairs a flat on wife, Janet's bike

ride. Every cyclist has their own preferred liquid replenishment as well as their preferred nutrition bar. Each cyclist's hydration and nutritional needs are different. Experiment with water, Gatorade, Powerbars, etc and you will learn what works best for you. Begin hydrating before you leave your house for a ride and continue drinking throughout your ride. We begin each ride with one bottle of water and another bottle with water and a dissolved NUUN® tablet. We find NUUN® to be a refreshing electrolyte replacement drink without the sugar of other hydration drinks. For more information about NUUN® hydration tablets, go to www.nuun.com. CamelBak packs are another effective method of carrying fluids, food, phones, cameras or anything else you may to carry. With their hoses and mouthpieces, CamelBaks tend to provide a safer way for a beginning rider to drink. The drawback of wearing a CamelBak is the weight on your back. Like anything else, it becomes a matter of preference. When we first began riding, we each carried a CamelBak, but now we rarely use them as we carry minimal supplies on our rides to reduce weight. The routes chosen for this book have plenty of places where you can replenish your water and food supplies.

Team In Training

Alice and Kevin at beautiful Lake Tahoe
during America's Most Beautiful Bike Ride 2005

We joined the Leukemia & Lymphoma Society's Team In Training® (TNT) when our son was diagnosed with Hodgkin's Lymphoma during his senior year of college. Through TNT, we met amazing people, made new friends, learned much about cycling, had a great time and helped raise money for blood cancer research. TNT is the largest endurance sports training program in the world. Through TNT, you can train for half-marathons, marathons, triathlons and century bike rides. We participated in the 2005 "America's Most Beautiful Bike Ride," a century ride around Lake Tahoe (Alice also ran the 2007 Rock 'N Roll

Marathon in San Diego, CA with TNT). We trained with certified trainers and coaches for four months. We had personalized web pages to assist in our fundraising. Most importantly, we had almost 70 committed teammates to help us through the difficult task of completing a Century ride. TNT participates in several Century rides each year. Go to www.teamintraining.org for more information.

Cyclists on America's Most Beautiful Bike Ride climb the mountain around Emerald Bay.

Cue Sheet Symbology

Before you head out to ride through northern Virginia's beautiful countryside, here is an explanation of the symbols used in the cue sheets. Normally there is a symbol below for each turn on the cue sheet. However, occasionally we had added extra descriptions to better prepare you for a section of a ride. For example, if a railroad crossing is at an angle on the road or is particularly rough, then we say "RR (angled)" so you can be ready to slow and take extra precaution at the crossing. We have **CAPITALIZED & BOLDED** certain notes for emphasis.

SS	Stop sign
TL	Traffic Light
YS	Yield Sign
4WS	Four way Stop (3WS is 3 way stop, etc)
T	T Intersection
L	Left Turn
R	Right Turn
S	Straight
SA	Straight across
TRO	To remain on
BR	Bear Right
BL	Bear Left
QL	Quick left turn
QR	Quick Right turn
X	Cross
RR	Railroad crossing
SR	State Road
Hwy	Highway
VBW	Virginia Byway
TRAFFIC	High Volume or High Speed Traffic
BEC	Becomes - road changes name

Ride Map Color Codes

We organized the colors on every map (except the Prince William Forest Park map in Chapter 2), as follows. The START/FINISH is always in red. The routes are always green. The directional arrows are in red. Significant streams, rivers or lakes are in blue as well as the names of the streams, rivers or lakes. All other locations are in basic black unless there is a special note or caution such as railroad crossings, which are also in red. Interstate signs depict Interstates and basic state highway signs depict major state highways.

Members of the National Capitol Chapter of the Leukemia and Lymphoma Society's Team in Training take a break from a training ride at Sugarloaf Mountain

Ride Difficulty Ranking & Details

In determining our difficulty ranking, we considered primarily the total mileage and total climbing on each ride. However we also considered specific climbs and our overall feeling of the rides as we do them. We are accustomed to riding on Skyline Drive and the rolling/not-so-rolling hills of the Shenandoah Valley. As we have ridden with friends who live in locations with differing topography, we have come to realize that our assessment of the difficulty of rides may be slightly skewed towards climbing. We have more difficulty when riding on flats than when riding on hills. We welcome your feedback and opinions.

1. **Skyline Drive: Mile 0 to Big Meadows** & return. 102 miles; 13,070 total feet of climbing; averages 128 feet of climbing per mile. See Chapter 9.

2. **Skyline Drive: Mile 0 to Thornton Gap** & return. 63 miles; 7,744 total feet of climbing; averages 123 feet of climbing per mile. See Chapter 9.

3. **Winchester Loop**: 63 miles. 4,136 total feet of climbing; averages 66 feet of climbing per mile. See Chapter 8.

4. **Skyline Drive: Thornton Gap Entrance to Big Meadows** & return: 39 miles; 5,326 total feet of climbing; averages 137 feet of climbing per mile. See Chapter 9.

5. **Reddish Knob**: 44 miles; 7,112 total feet of climbing; averages 162 feet of climbing per mile. See Chapter 14.

6. **Mount Weather**: 48 miles; 4,487 total feet of climbing; averages 93 feet of climbing per mile. See Chapter 4.

7. **Todd Lake**: 48 miles; 4,292 total feet of climbing; averages 89 feet of climbing per mile. See Chapter 14.

8. **The Plains**: 54 miles; 3,841 total feet of climbing; averages 71 feet of climbing per mile. See Chapter 3.

9. **Fort Valley Loop**: 55 miles; 2,218 total feet of climbing; averages 40 feet of climbing per mile. See Chapter 7.

10. **Harrisonburg Loop**: 44 miles; 5,012 total feet of climbing; averages 114 feet of climbing per mile. See Chapter 13.

11. **Middletown Loop**: 48 miles; 3,180 total feet of climbing; averages 66 feet of climbing per mile. See Chapter 6.

12. **Luray Loop**: 36 miles; 3,255 total feet of climbing; averages 90 feet of climbing per mile. See Chapter 11.

13. **Edinburg Loop**: 40 miles; 3,503 total feet of climbing; averages 88 feet of climbing per mile. See Chapter 10.

14. **New Market Loop**: 41 miles; 3,066 total feet of climbing; averages 75 feet of climbing per mile. See Chapter 12.

15. **Broadway Loop**: 36 miles; 2,463 total feet of climbing; averages 68 feet of climbing per mile. See Chapter 12.

16. **Meems Bottom Covered Bridge**: 36 miles; 2,299 total feet of climbing; averages 64 feet of climbing per mile. See Chapter 12.

17. **Cedar Creek Battlefield**: 30 miles; 2,102 total feet of climbing; averages 70 feet of climbing per mile. See Chapter 7.

18. **Burwell-Morgan Mill**: 29 miles; 1,869 total feet of climbing; averages 64 feet of climbing per mile. See Chapter 5.

19. **Prince William Forest Park**: 25 miles; 1,830 total feet of climbing; averages 73 feet of climbing per mile. See Chapter 2.

2

Prince William Forest Park

How to Get There (where to park)

Prince William Forest Park Entrance

Getting to Prince William Forest Park is easy - just take Exit 150B on Interstate 95. If traveling South on I-95 take exit 150B to the right. As you take the exit to the right there is a Yield sign and you are only allowed to continue straight on Highway 619 West. Use caution as the merge distance is limited and traffic coming from your left normally is moving fast. Stay in the right hand lane - it has the right turn arrow - and you stay straight past one right turn and then come to the Park entrance to the right. Total distance from the 150B exit to the turn into the Park is approximately 1/4 mile. If traveling North on I-95, take exit 150 and go Left at the bottom of the ramp onto Highway 619 West; then follow the directions above.

There is a Park Ranger shed where you must stop and pay your $5 entry fee per vehicle; $3 if entering on your bike without a vehicle; and $20 for an annual pass (includes pass holder and occupants of vehicle - 14 passengers or less). If the Ranger shed at the Park entrance is closed there will be a sign directing you to the Visitor's Center to pay your entry fee. The Visitor Center is approximately 1/2 mile from the Park entrance. At either location, the Ranger will offer you a map and we highly recommend obtaining a map if you have never been to Prince William Forest Park. The Ranger gives you a receipt to tape it to your windshield when parking so the Rangers know you have paid. Of course, if you show the Ranger your Annual Interagency Pass they just give you a parking receipt, and offer you a map.

There is excellent signage within Prince William Forest Park and many parking areas beginning with the Pine Grove picnic and parking area adjacent to the Visitor Center. You may continue past the Visitor Center for approximately another 1/2 mile to the Telegraph Picnic area. The Visitor Center, Pine Grove picnic area and Telegraph picnic area all have restrooms. The Visitor Center is air-conditioned - a welcome relief on muggy summer afternoons!

There is ample parking along the Scenic Drive with Parking Areas listed as "A" through "H." Each parking area connects you with a hiking trail that is also listed on the parking area sign. Parking areas A through C are located before you come to the Scenic Drive loop proper. Parking area D is our recommended parking area for riding within Prince William Forest Park. It is the last parking area where you can stop without committing yourself to driving your vehicle along the entire Scenic Drive 7.3 mile loop. Scenic Drive becomes one-way for vehicular traffic for 3.3 miles beginning at parking area D. There are 22 parking spaces in parking area D - one of which is handicap parking.

Lay o' The Land

Located approximately 20 miles south of the D.C. Beltway is an absolute jewel of an area for safe, enjoyable road biking. One of more than 380 parks in the U.S. Department of the Interior's National Park System, Prince William Forest Park has over 15,000 acres of Piedmont Forest woodland. Though the park entrance is less than 1/2 mile from I-95, you generally feel as if you are deep inside a forested sanctuary - miles away from civilization. The road network in Prince William Forest Park is wooded, secluded and feels as if you riding along Skyline Drive in the Shenandoah National Park or along the Blue Ridge Parkway. The roadways are generally winding, curving, and slanting downward and upward into shade covered turns in the road. There are false flats where you dig into the pedals as the road gives you just enough feedback to push a little harder. On the other hand, if riding in the opposite direction along the same stretch of road, you feel the road slipping away beneath you as you crank progressively bigger gears until you are riding along with the roar of the wind in your ears sounding like waves rushing to the shore along the beach. On most rides in Prince William Forest Park, you will probably see deer, turkey, squirrels, rabbits, foxes and possibly bear! In fact, you have to pay attention to the road, as you never know when some wild animal may dart into your path!

Adding to the feeling of "being away" is the low usage rate of the park - especially when you consider many visitors come to hike the trails. There is little vehicular traffic within Prince William Forest Park. The maximum speed limit is 35 MPH with a 25 MPH limit on the 3.3-mile section of road in the 7.3-mile loop allowing only one-way vehicular traffic in the right lane. The left lane of the road is divided into two lanes for foot, bicycle, and roller blade traffic. In road segments through the various campgrounds, the speed limit is 10 MPH. If you want the park completely to yourself, then visit on a weekday morning - Kevin once took half a day off work, rode 60 miles in the morning, and only saw two Park Ranger vehicles during the entire time! Of course, the low density of vehicles coupled with the great natural beauty of the park can create its own hazards by lulling you into an almost unconscious state of being one with the forest - until of course you hear the honk of a horn behind you!

On weekends, you can expect to have a higher density of visitors as the park is a popular place for Boy Scouts and Girl Scouts to camp and/or hike on weekends. Prince William Forest Park also has ideal terrain for Orienteering and hosts several meets each year. Though you always want to follow safe riding procedures, you must be especially vigilant on weekends with the increased number of park visitors. We have found that it is best to assume the walkers, joggers, roller bladders and indeed the other cyclists do not know the basic rules of passing on the left (do not be surprised if your announcing of passing, "On your left," has no effect) and walking, etc on the right - especially along the 3.3 mile section. When coming upon a family of four or five on bikes or walking their dogs along the pedestrian section we have found the safest thing to do is to ensure the one-way vehicular lane is clear and just pass in that lane (though still announcing we are passing if coming from behind a group). Always give dogs on leashes plenty of room so the dog does not suddenly dart into your path while chasing a squirrel or rabbit. Frankly, we recommend the bigger the dog the farther away you announce your presence so the dog's owner can get a good grip on the leash!

Unlike many of the other rides described in this book that generally take you along a circuitous loop with limited sections of roadway ridden more than once, riding in Prince William Forest Park consists of a single 2.3 mile "out-and-back" ride connecting the Park entrance to a 7.3 mile loop. Some turn-off roads provide variety to any route, allowing you to mix and match segments into a longer ride that seemingly takes you into new territory with each new turn of the road.

Other unique features of Prince William Forest Park are the many restrooms, pay phones, and water fountains available.

Visitor's Center & Country Store

The Oakridge Campground even has showers with hot and cold running water year-round. Telegraph Picnic Area, the Visitor Center & Country Store, Pine Grove Picnic Area, Turkey Run Education Center and Oakridge Campground all have restrooms and potable water available. The Visitor Center & Country Store, Turkey Run Education Center and Oakridge Campground all have pay telephones and soft drink machines should you get tired of your water bottle!

Ride Description

All of the major roads were recently paved (as of February 2012) making your ride incredibly smooth. The primary road within Prince William Forest Park is simply - and aptly - named "Scenic Drive." Scenic Drive begins by taking a left 0.4 miles from the Park entrance. Scenic Drive runs for approximately two miles where you have an option to take a left towards Turkey Run Ridge or stay straight on Scenic Drive. Staying straight takes you on the full 7.3 mile Scenic Drive loop. Approximately 0.4 miles after passing the turn to Turkey Run, you find Parking Area "D" on your left. Parking Area D is the last opportunity to stop and park without committing to driving the entire 7.3-mile loop. Immediately after Parking Area D, Scenic Drive becomes one-way vehicular traffic in the right lane and two-way pedestrian traffic in the left lane for approximately 3.2 miles to the turn towards Oakridge Campground. The campground has parking for 13 vehicles (one for handicap parking) at the entrance to the campground and 100 campsites broken into three sections (A, B, & C). The 1-way camp road that loops through each section has the roughest road surface in the park - watch out for potholes, gravel, and branches that may have fallen onto the road.

If you take Scenic Drive to the left towards Turkey Run Ridge, you can drive for approximately 3.6 miles to a left towards Oakridge Campground but you cannot continue the Scenic Drive loop as you run into the one-way vehicular and pedestrian roadway. As explained previously, riding in Prince William Forest Park entails combining differing roadway segments into a multiple of ride combinations to achieve your desired mileage. For example, the first Century ride Kevin ever completed was achieved by completing a mind numbing 16 loops of the 3.3 road up to the turn to Oakridge Road and then a short 1/2 mile segment to get to the Century mark. We enjoy riding loops around the 7.3 mile Scenic Drive - alternating directions for a change of scenery. In fact, we measure many of our other rides by computing how many "Prince William loops" they contain. Alice always knows she can complete "one more Prince William loop" if we are riding a difficult longer route elsewhere.

Prince William Forest Park – 25 miles

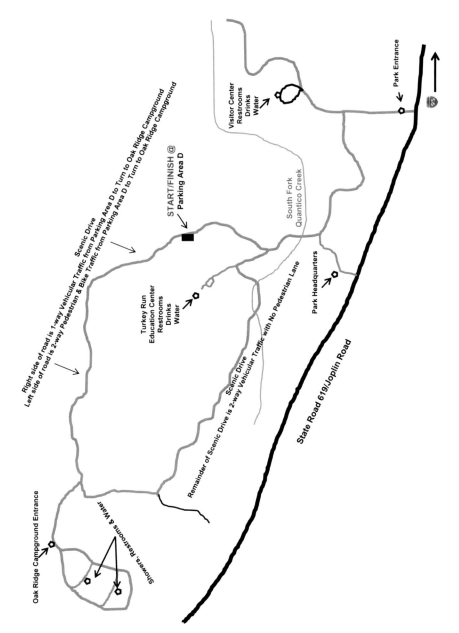

Park Entrance

Visitor Center
Restrooms
Drinks
Water

Scenic Drive
Right side of road is 1-way Vehicular Traffic from Parking Area D to Turn to Oak Ridge Campground
Left side of road is 2-way Pedestrian & Bike Traffic from Parking Area D to Turn to Oak Ridge Campground

START/FINISH @
Parking Area D

South Fork
Quantico Creek

Turkey Run
Education Center
Restrooms
Drinks
Water

Park Headquarters

Scenic Drive
Remainder of Scenic Drive is 2-way Vehicular Traffic with No Pedestrian Lane

State Road 619/Joplin Road

Oak Ridge Campground Entrance

Showers, Restrooms & Water

~ Refer to page 10 for Ride Map Color Codes ~

Prince William Forest Park Cue Sheet

Cue Sheet for approximately 25-mile Ride
Beginning at Parking Area D

	Total	Segment
L out of Parking Area "D"		3.3
R on Oakridge Rd; follow 1-way route thru campground & return along Oakridge Rd to **SS**	3.3	2.2
R on Scenic Drive	5.5	3.2
L on Turkey Run Rd; turn around in parking lot; circle through Turkey Run Group Campground; **R** on Turkey Run Rd to **SS**	8.7	0.8
L on Scenic Drive to **SS**	9.5	0.3
R on Scenic Drive towards Park Exit	9.8	1.9
R @ **SS** towards Park Exit, loop around and continue to Telegraph Picnic area; continue thru the Telegraph picnic area and loop back towards Park Exit	11.7	1.9
R on Scenic Drive	13.6	1.9
L on Scenic Drive towards Turkey Run Ridge	15.5	0.3
R on Turkey Run Rd & circle thru as before	15.8	0.8
R on Scenic Drive	16.4	3.2
L on Oakridge Rd; loop thru Oakridge Campground and return as before	19.6	2.2
L @ **SS** on Scenic Drive	21.8	3.3
R into Parking Area "D"	25.2	

~ Refer to page 9 for Cue Sheet Symbology ~

Prince William Forest Park Elevation Profile
Start: 290 ft   Low: 150 ft   High: 429 ft
Total Gain: 1,830 ft   Distance: 25 mi
Average Elevation Gain: 73 ft/mile

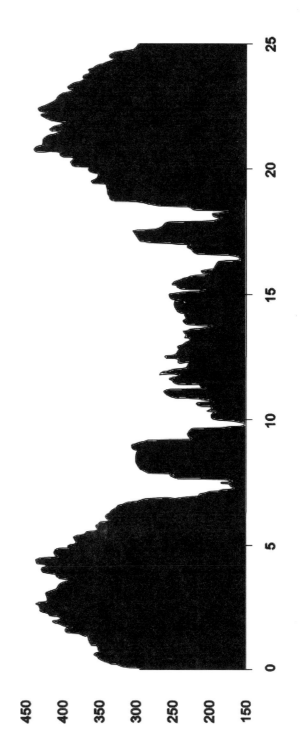

Places to Eat

The best place for a variety of restaurants, take I-95 North either up to the Potomac Mills Mall area or to the Prince William Parkway area. Follow signs to Potomac Mills Mall off exit 156 and take exit 158 to get to the many restaurants along the Prince William Parkway west of I-95.

Local Bike Shops

The closest bike shop to Prince William Forest Park is a Revolution Cycles store (2773 Jefferson Davis Highway; 540-657-6900) in Stafford. Additionally there is an Olde Towne Bicycles store (14477 Potomac Mills Road; 703-491-5700) located near Potomac Mills Mall.

Revolution Cycles Peloton on their monthly staff ride. Chris Meier leads Peter Nugyen, Alex Heymann & Caleb Chik; then Nate Lohmeier leads Mike Hamannwright & Jakob Wolf-Barnett

Local Attractions

Prince William Forest Park itself is a destination attraction for many people within the Metro D.C. area. Along with its excellent paved roads, there are many dirt roads available for mountain bike and trails for hiking throughout the Park. Quantico National Cemetery is practically across the road from the Park entrance - just continue past the Park entrance for one mile until you come to the Cemetery entrance on the left. Bicycles are prohibited in Quantico National Cemetery. Without doubt, the biggest local attraction is Potomac Mills Mall - the most popular attraction in the state of Virginia! Potomac Mills Mall is six miles north along I-95. Potomac Mills is a shopping Mecca. You can find anything and everything either in Potomac Mills Mall itself or the surrounding strip malls.

3

The Plains

How to Get There (where to park)

We begin this ride in the Village of The Plains, Virginia established in 1831. To get to The Plains from the Metro D.C. area, take I-66 West from the I-66 and I-495 Interchange to Exit 31. At the bottom of the exit, go Right on Hwy 245 North for one mile to the "T" intersection of Hwy 245 and Hwy 55. Just before the intersection, there are parking spaces on both sides of the road and there are normally open spaces on weekends (especially Sunday) in The Plains Pharmacy parking lot on the left. If traveling from the I-81 corridor, take I-66 East to Exit 31.

Forlano's Market is a welcome sight as you turn right onto Hwy 55 West at the end of the ride.

Approximately five miles before Exit 31 you pass through Thoroughfare Gap in the Bull Run Mountains, crossing Broad Run on I-66 as you transit Thoroughfare Gap. Thoroughfare Gap was the site of an August 28, 1862 Civil War skirmish that, of itself was a minor affair yet because of Confederate Lieutenant General Longstreet's success enabled him to link up with General Lee's Army at the Second battle of Manassas August 29-30, 1862. Longstreet's forces were instrumental in the defeat of Federal Major General John Pope's forces. Nowadays Thoroughfare Gap marks the beginning of the rolling hill country so characteristic of northern Virginia's horse country. At the bottom of the Exit 31 ramp, you see distinctive green barns with white trim that host a Farmers Market every Sunday from 10:00 a.m. until 3:00 p.m. from May to October. You will find fresh produce, freshly baked goodies, drinks, sandwiches and various local crafts at the market - a good post-ride stop! Within The Plains, there is a BP gas station/deli that carries a nice selection of power/energy bars and it has a functional "his & her" bathroom. Another post-ride or pre-ride option is Forlano's Market located at the Hwy 245 & Hwy 55 intersection serving lunch seven days a week and dinner Wednesday through Saturday.

Lay o' the Land

While all of the rides in this book are favorites of ours, this 54 mile ride - "The Plains" is special because it was the first ride we took together out onto the roads of northern Virginia. Longtime friend, Bob Marsh accompanied us on that ride and was instrumental in our completing it as we had some "mechanical difficulties" along the way due to falls. There is nothing like a fall to impress on your mind the importance of clipping out before coming to a stop - especially on an uphill! This ride might be better described as the "Tour of north central Fauquier County" since we ride across most of beautiful Fauquier County's horse country north and west of Warrenton, with a brief soirée into Prince William County. Be prepared for seeing huge estates with terrific views of the northern Virginia countryside. You will experience everything from completely open roadways surrounded by pasture and farmland to completely shaded roadways through dense forests. The hills are mostly longer rollers but there is a steep climb near the end as you cross the Bull Run Mountains on SR 601 that may get you up out of the saddle.

Ride Description

This ride is characterized by long, rolling climbs followed by equally long down hills. The rolling hills are can normally only be powered over by the strongest of cyclists. Most of us mortals will gear down near our "Granny-gear" as we crest the tops. Establishing a solid cadence is the name of the game for this ride! Begin by taking a Left onto Hwy 55 West watching out for the first of several railroad crossings after just 1/10th of a mile. Hwy 55 is a narrow, predominantly two-lane rural highway with little shoulder and high-speed traffic so use caution whenever on Hwy 55. There is a triple railroad crossing at four miles as you enter the town of Marshall. Marshall has several eating establishments and bathrooms. By the time you reach Marshall you will have already seen the large, stately homes that characterize those along the entire ride. Large acreages of both pasture and croplands line the entire route.

The ride continues by taking a Left at mile 6.4 miles onto Ramey Road (SR 732). You will find some rollers as you climb onto the shoulders of Little Cobbler Mountain enroute to riding halfway around Big Cobbler Mountain before taking a Right onto Hume Rd (SR 635) after 10.8 miles. Stay straight on Hume Rd until the Stop sign at Leeds Manor Rd (SR 688) in the Village of Hume. There is one of those long climbs promised during the last mile or so to the turn at Leeds Manor Rd. You will see some excellent post-ride options in the village of Hume, as there are directional signs for some Virginia Wineway Vineyards, Philip Carter Winery and Rappahannock Cellars. More about the vineyards later! At approximately mile 20 in the Village of Orlean you come to the Orlean Market on the left. The Orlean Market is open seven days a week serving freshly prepared deli sandwiches, hand-dipped ice cream and drinks - also a clean bathroom! The Orlean Market has sufficient parking to begin and end your ride from there.

The Orlean Market
is a great place to take a food, drink or bathroom break!

Continue on Leeds Manor Rd for another 5.5 miles and take a Left onto Old Waterloo Rd (SR 691) at mile 25.6. After two miles (with some steep down hills!), stay on Old Waterloo Rd by taking a Right onto SR 678. Stay on Old Waterloo Rd all the way to the sharp corner where the Howard Johnson's is on the left. You have now entered Warrenton where you find plenty of places to stop for a bite to eat during your ride and for a post-ride celebration! However, you must carefully negotiate its narrow, hilly, heavily trafficked streets for almost two miles. It is safest to dismount and walk your bike across this very busy intersection of Hwy 211 and Business Hwy 29 South. Cross the intersection onto Waterloo Street and stay on Waterloo to the top of the hill (be careful getting into the left turn lane) and take a Left onto Alexandria Pike (steep downhill). After almost 1/2-mile stay straight onto Blackwell Rd as Alexandria Pike goes right. Stay straight on Blackwell Rd across the busy intersection of Business Hwy 29 and Business Hwy 15. There is a Sheetz gas station on the left at this

Beth Turner
enjoying her ride along
Old Waterloo Road.

intersection - making it a good place for a bathroom break and drink. For most of the next almost two miles Blackwell Rd is a very narrow road with some twisting down hills before taking a Left at mile 35 and then an immediate Right to remain on Blackwell Rd.

You will be treated to over two miles of some of the prettiest land in northern Virginia as you continue on Blackwell Rd to the Stop sign at mile 37.2 where you take a Right onto Blantyre Rd (SR 628). Stay on Blantyre Rd and when it becomes Georgetown Rd follow it all the way to the Stop sign at Hwy 55 at mile 41.9. Take a Right onto Hwy 55 East and stay on Hwy 55 East for approximately four miles to a Left on Antioch Rd (SR 681) - mile 45.9. You cross into Prince William County as you cross Broad Run in Thoroughfare gap. There is an angled railroad crossing about one mile before the Antioch Rd turn in Thoroughfare, VA so use caution. Stay on Antioch Rd - you immediately cross over I-66 - until the Stop sign at mile 48.8. Go left onto Waterfall Rd (SR 601). You begin the final climb over Bull Run Mountain about one mile before you come to Waterfall Rd. The steepest climb begins about 1/2 mile after getting on Waterfall Rd and crests at mile 50.3 - WHEW! You re-enter Fauquier County during the climb and Waterfall Rd changes to Hopewell Rd at mile 49.8. Stay on Hopewell for just over two miles and you re-enter The Plains. Take a Left onto Loudoun Ave at mile 53.8 - careful of the railroad tracks im-

View of barn, pasture, and house on hill along Blackwell Road

mediately after going left! Go to the Stop sign at take a Right on Hwy 55 West and then finish the ride by taking a Left onto Hwy 245 South at the intersection. After this ride, you have earned a great meal and we have a variety of recommendations for you.

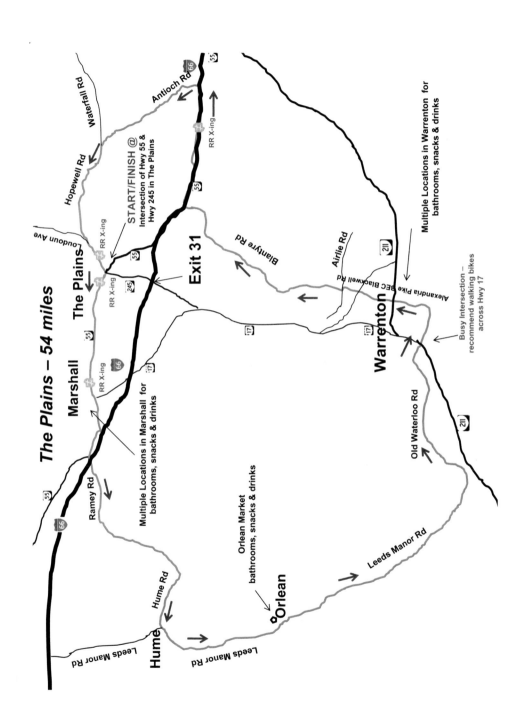

The Plains – 54 miles

START/FINISH @ Intersection of Hwy 55 & Hwy 245 in The Plains

Exit 31

The Plains

Marshall

Warrenton

Orlean

Hume

Waterfall Rd

Hopewell Rd

Antioch Rd

Loudoun Ave

Blantyre Rd

Airlie Rd

Alexandria Pike BEC Blackwell Rd

Old Waterloo Rd

Leeds Manor Rd

Ramey Rd

Hume Rd

Leeds Manor Rd

Leeds Manor Rd

RR X-ing

Multiple Locations in Warrenton for bathrooms, snacks & drinks

Busy Intersection – recommend walking bikes across Hwy 17

Multiple Locations in Marshall for bathrooms, snacks & drinks

Orlean Market bathrooms, snacks & drinks

~ Refer to page 10 for Ride Map Color Codes ~

The Plains Cue Sheet

	Total	Segment
L on Hwy 55 West		0.1
RR	0.1	2.7
Northern Fauquier Community Park on right	2.8	1.2
3RR	4.0	2.4
L on Ramey Rd (SR 732)	6.4	4.4
R on Hume Rd (SR 635)	10.8	3.2
L on Leeds Manor Rd (SR 688)	14.0	5.9
Orlean Market on left	19.9	5.6
L on Old Waterloo Rd (SR 691)	25.5	1.9
R on Wilson Rd (SR 678) **BEC** Old Waterloo Rd	27.4	4.0
Old Waterloo Rd ends. **SA** intersection of Hwy 211 and Hwy 17 onto Waterloo St. **CAUTION**	31.4	0.7
L on Alexandria Pike; **BEC** Blackwell Rd	32.1	1.0
SA Hwy 211 **TRO** Blackwell Rd	33.1	1.7
L onto Airlie Rd	34.8	0.0
QR to remain on Blackwell Rd (SR 672)	34.8	2.4
R on Blantyre Rd (SR 628)	37.2	4.3
BL TRO Blantyre Rd (SR 674)	41.5	0.2
R on Hwy 55 East	41.7	3.0
RR	44.7	1.0
L on Antioch Rd	45.7	2.5
The Winery @ **La Grange** on left	48.2	0.6
L on Waterfall Rd (SR601); **BEC** Hopewell Rd	48.8	5.0
L on Loudoun Ave (SR 626); immediate **RR**	53.8	0.0
R on Hwy 55 West (50 yds to end of ride)	54.0	

~ Refer to page 9 for Cue Sheet Symbology ~

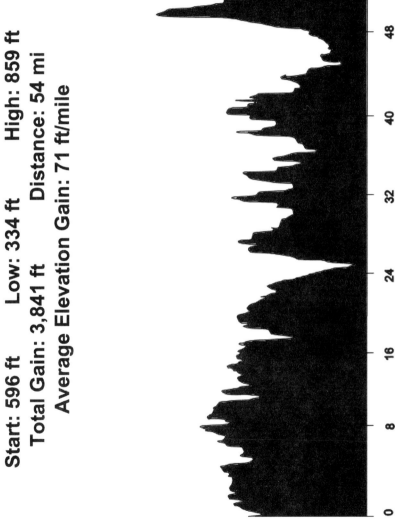

The Plains Elevation Profile

Start: 596 ft   Low: 334 ft   High: 859 ft

Total Gain: 3,841 ft   Distance: 54 mi

Average Elevation Gain: 71 ft/mile

Places to eat

There are many eating options on this ride. Forlano's Market, located at 6483 Main Street (540) 253-5456 serves fresh deli sandwiches and cold drinks! As mentioned in the ride description, The Orlean Market located at the intersection of Leeds Manor Rd/Rt 688, (540) 364-7339 serves terrific deli sandwiches with generous portions of everything - meals of themselves!

Additionally, there are any number of fast food chain restaurants in Warrenton as well as several local eateries in Marshall.

Local Bike Shop

The Bike Stop at 61 South 4th St, Warrenton (540) 341-7702 is the closest bike shop along this ride. They feature a full-service repair shop. Hours are Mon-Sat 9:30 a.m. - 6:00 p.m.; Sun 12:00 p.m. - 5:00 p.m.

Local Attractions

Unless you happen to ride on a day when there is a local event occurring, the biggest attractions would have to be the several excellent wineries in the area. Listed in no particular order are some of the wineries closer to the route. The Virginia wine industry is growing with additional wineries opening frequently so you may also find other wineries near the riding area. Most of the wineries offer tours and tastings along with some cheeses or other foods to go with the wine. You may to consider altering the cue sheet to begin and end your ride at a winery! We recommend you coordinate with the winery before doing so!

Philip Carter Winery of Virginia. Open daily April -November 11:00 a.m. - 6:00 p.m. December - March Thursday-Monday 11:00 a.m. - 6:00 p.m. (540) 364-1203. www.pcwinery.com

Rappahannock Cellars. Open daily all year 10:30 a.m. - 5:00 p.m. Sat 10:30 a.m. - 6:00 p.m. (540) 635-9398. www.rappahannockcellars.com

The Winery at La Grange. Open daily 11:00 a.m. - 6:00 p.m. (703) 753-9360. www.wineryatlagrange.com

Piedmont Vineyards and Winery. Open daily April - October 11:00 a.m. - 6:00 p.m.; November - March 11:00 a.m. - 5:00 p.m. (540) 687-5528. www.piedmontwines.com

Pearmund Cellars. Open daily 10:00 a.m. - 6:00 p.m. (540) 347-3475. www.pearmundcellars.com

Naked Mountain Winery & Vineyards. Open daily 11:00 a.m. - 5:00 p.m.; closed Thanksgiving Day, December 24th - 26th & 31st and New Year's Day. www.nakedmtnwinery.com

Barrel Oak Winery. Open Sunday - Thursday 11:00 a.m. - 6:00 p.m.; Friday 11:00 a.m. - 9:00 p.m.; Saturday 11:00 a.m. - 6:00 p.m. (540) 364-6402. www.barreloak.com

Miracle Valley Vineyard. Open Thursday - Monday 11:00 a.m. - 5:00 p.m. (540) 364-0228. www.miraclevalleyvineyard.com

Three Fox Vineyards. Open Friday - Sunday 12:00 p.m. - 6:00 p.m. or by appointment from April 21st - December 17th. (540) 364-6073. www.threefoxvineyards.com

*Friends Eric & Jen Mortimer with Alice & Kevin
enjoying a tasting at Barrel Oak Winery*

*Visit 3 Fox Vineyards and get a warm welcome
from owners Holli & John Todhunter!*

4

Middleburg (Mount Weather)

Middleburg is a quaint little town in the middle of Virginia horse country. Easily accessible and with many things to do après' ride, Middleburg is our favorite start point for this fun but challenging ride. Though we begin and end the ride in Middleburg the salient feature of this ride is Mount Weather. The climb up the mountain is challenging; the ride along the ridgeline is beautiful; and the ride down the southern end of the mountain is thrilling.

The Mount Weather climb from the bottom
(this picture does not show the steepness of the climb!)

How to Get There (where to park)

From the D.C. Beltway take I-66 West to Exit 57 and get on Hwy 50 West. Stay on Hwy 50 West for approximately 23 miles to Middleburg. Turn Right at the first (only) light onto North Madison St for a short distance and stay to the right to stay on North Madison St and you come to Middleburg Elementary School on your right. There is normally plenty of parking unless it is a nice day for biking because you then may find the parking lot fun of fellow cycling enthusiasts! Upon entering Middleburg, there is an Exxon station on your right that sells drinks and has bathrooms. One block past the traffic light on the right is a Safeway grocery store that also has bathrooms - as well as drinks and snacks for the ride! While driving along Hwy 50

West to Middleburg for this ride, be mindful of the several small towns you pass through and the sudden changes in speed limits! Traveling east on I-66, take Exit 31 and go North on Hwy 245 to The Plains. Go Right on Hwy 55 East at the "T" intersection and then Left on Hwy 626 to Middleburg.

Lay o' the Land

Situated in the middle of Virginia's breathtakingly beautiful horse country, the Mount Weather ride is both challenging and rewarding. Riders will notice five distinct sections along this almost 49-mile ride. The ride from the Middleburg Elementary School parking lot to Bluemont is characterized by narrow, hilly, winding, sunken roads, lined by stonewall fences large pastures and large homes. The SR 601 section up Mount Weather, along its ridgeline and down the mountain is characterized by forests close to each side of the road and overhanging the road in many cases. The section through Crooked Run Valley is open pastureland, on a wide, flat road and closely monitored speed limits for vehicular traffic. From Hwy 17 to Zulla Rd the route becomes a mirror of the initial section - narrow, hilly, winding roads with large pastures and homes lining the road. The Zulla Rd section is long, straight and relatively flat back to Hwy 50 and into Middleburg.

Ride Description

This ride has something for everyone - and we are not just talking about the many things to see and do in an afternoon in Middleburg! There are climbs, descents, flats, curves, and straights. Wildlife abounds throughout the ride. Bring your camera to take advantage of the many picturesque views on this ride.

As explained above this ride has five distinctly different sections to it. Exiting the Middleburg Elementary School parking lot, you quickly experience the narrow, hilly, winding road characteristic of many of the Virginia Byways. The hills tend to be short but they bring you out of the saddle! This section of the ride never becomes rolling to the point where your momentum carries over the next hill while staying seated. It can remind you of some of the spinning classes where the leader has you jumping up on the pedals and then sprinting down the backside after cresting the hill! At about mile 2.3, bear right to remain on Foxcroft Rd. After getting on St Louis Rd, you have almost four miles of short hills until you turn Left on Snickersville Rd. At about mile 10.4 there is a small market on the right corner of the road at the Stop sign. The store has a porta-john behind it - perfect for those who had too much coffee on the ride out to Middleburg.

*Bluemont General Store
- a welcome stop*

Three miles further, you come to Bluemont and more importantly, the Bluemont General Store. With a wide selection of organic goodies and drinks, the Bluemont General Store is your last chance to pick up food on this ride. There is also a clean porta-john behind the general store. Having mentioned all the reasons to stop at the Bluemont General Store, we will now tell you why you do not want to linger too long. There is an almost half-mile climb from the Bluemont General Store up to Hwy 7; followed by another half-mile of uphill along Hwy 7 West before you get to the challenging half-mile climb up Mount Weather immediately followed by a lesser climb over half a mile to the ridgeline of Mount Weather.

Once you reach the ridgeline of Mount Weather, you have a relatively flat ride for several miles before the three-mile descent off the mountain to cross Hwy 50 at Ashby Gap. There is only one section of the descent where you have to pedal up a rise for about 200 yards. Blueridge Mountain Road (SR 601) is an absolutely beautiful road with what appear to be second homes secluded in the deep woods back from the road. Many sections of the road are completely overhung by trees - making it a cooler ride in the late spring and summer. Be especially careful in the early fall though as leaves will be on the road and are very slippery!

A note of caution - you cross Hwy 7 twice and Hwy 50 once getting onto and off Mount Weather. Both Hwy 7 and Hwy 50 are a four lane high-speed highways where the route crosses them. We strongly recommend walking your bike across the highways each time you cross them.

The ride on Hwy 17 (Winchester Rd) through Crooked Run Valley is incredible and certainly worthy of its Virginia Byway designation! In 1999, Scenic America named the valley and surrounding area one of America's "Last Chance Landscapes," and in 2000, the Preservation Alliance of Virginia called the view from Ashby's Gap towards Paris the "quintessential Virginia vista."

This almost eight-mile section of the ride has an excellent road surface, wide shoulders and a strictly imposed 45-mph speed limit on vehicular traffic. There are several destination locations on this short scenic section of the ride - so much so that you may be tempted to only ride through Crooked Run Valley!

1.3 miles along Hwy 17, there is an opportunity for a short side trip to the Sky Meadows State Park. The Visitor Center is just over one mile off Hwy 17 and has restrooms and water available as well a picnic area. Though there is a $4/day vehicle entrance fee, bicyclists are normally not charged unless there

Crooked Run Valley seen from Ashby Gap

is a special event - such as the Annual Delaplane Strawberry Festival on Memorial Day weekend. The park is open daily from 8:00 a.m. to dusk and could be used as a beginning point for this ride - complete with picnic afterwards in the park!

If you are looking for another detour, albeit a challenging one, then a short distance further down the road on the right from the entrance to Sky Meadows State Park is Leeds Manor Rd. Stay on Leeds Manor Rd for almost five miles to get to Naked Mountain Vineyard & Winery. Leeds Manor Rd is also a Virginia Byway so the beauty of the ride more than compensates for the challenges of this detour! The opportunities continue on the tour through Crooked Run Valley as the entrance to the boutique family winery - Delaplane Cellars is on the left at mile 30.4. The entrance to Three Fox Vineyards is on the right just before the RR crossing at mile 32.8.

As you turn off Hwy 17 onto Maidstone Rd you will see a sign for Barrel Oak Winery and Miracle Valley Vineyard. Maidstone Rd begins another eight-mile stretch of winding, curvy, hilly roads through large, fenced pastures and huge houses until the turn onto Zulla Rd. We have seen bald eagles soaring along this stretch! At mile 37 is the entrance Vintage Ridge Vineyard. Be careful not to miss the turn onto Frogtown Rd (SR 702) at about mile 39. There is no Stop sign or traffic light so this is an easy turn to miss.

The final six miles or so of the ride is along Zulla Rd. Compared to the rest of this ride, Zulla Rd is straight and less hilly than other sections of the ride. However, the surface of Zulla Rd is rough with many temporary patches, holes, and rough sections of pavement. Be careful or you may get a pinch flat (or two!) along Zulla Rd. Turning Right on Hwy 50, it is a short ride back into Middleburg and the Elementary School parking lot.

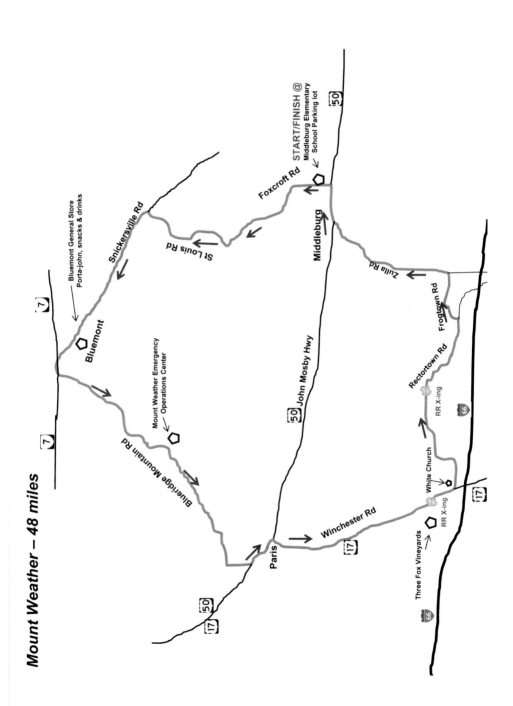

Mount Weather – 48 miles

Mount Weather Cue Sheet

	Total	Segment
R out of school parking lot on Foxcroft Rd (SR 626)		2.3
BR TRO Foxcroft Rd	2.3	1.3
Stay straight **TRO** Foxcroft Rd	3.6	0.9
R on St Louis Rd (SR 611)	4.5	3.6
L on Snickersville Rd (SR 734) **VBW**	8.1	2.3
SA @ **SS**; Market on corner (porta-john)	10.4	3.0
Bluemont General Store on left; (porta-john)	13.4	0.7
L on Harry Byrd Hwy (Hwy 7 West) **TRAFFIC**	14.1	0.5
L on Blueridge Mountain Rd (SR 601); **Climb**	14.6	4.4
Mount Weather Emergency Operations Center	19.0	6.3
L on Hwy 50 East **TRAFFIC**	25.3	1.2
R on Winchester Rd (Hwy 17 South) **VBW**	26.5	3.9
Delaplane Cellars on left	30.4	2.4
RR; Three Fox Vineyards on right	32.8	1.1
L on Maidstone Rd (SR 713) White Church on corner	33.9	2.6
RR	36.5	0.5
Vintage Ridge Vineyards on right	37.0	0.4
R on Rectortown Rd (SR 710)	37.4	1.3
L on Frogtown Rd (SR 702); **VBW**	38.7	2.3
BEC Rock Hill Mill Rd	41.0	1.1
L on Zulla Rd (SR 709)	42.1	4.7
R on John Mosby Hwy (Hwy 50 East) **TRAFFIC**	46.8	1.3
L on Madison St @ **TL**	48.1	0.1
Middleburg Elementary School on right	48.2	

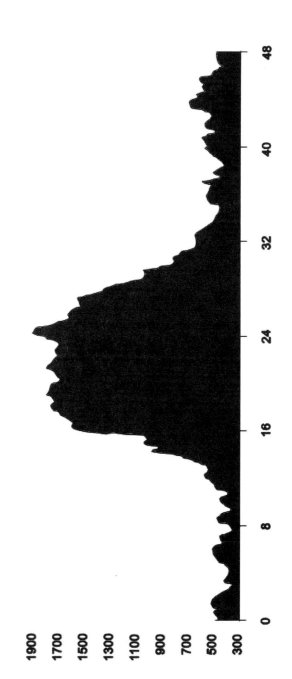

Mount Weather Elevation Profile
Start: 500 ft   Low: 331 ft   High: 1,886 ft
Total Gain: 4,487 ft   Distance: 48 mi
Average Elevation Gain: 93 ft/mile

Places to Eat

Between the restaurants near the route and Middleburg's offering of food establishments, you will find something for every budget, dress code and palate. Our favorite for a tasty meal after the ride is Teddy's Pizza & Subs at 9 East Federal St (one block off Washington St). Quick service, friendly staff and generous slices of pizza with fresh ingredients works for us!

Teddy's Pizza & Subs -
a great post-ride choice!

Local Bike Shops

As of this printing, we have not found a local bike shop in Middleburg or along the route. Therefore, we recommend you go to your local bike shop for any adjustments your bike may require before heading out on this ride. Within the group, you should always the basics for minor repairs such as cable adjustments and flat tires.

Local Attractions

Unless you go to Middleburg's web page (www.middleburgonline.com) to locate a specific event, the primary attractions would have to be the several excellent wineries in the area. Listed in no particular order are some of the wineries closer to the route. The Virginia wine industry is growing with additional wineries opening frequently so you may also find other wineries near the riding area. Most of the wineries offer tours and tastings (many free!) along with some cheeses or other foods to go with the wine. You may to consider altering the cue sheet to begin and end your ride at a winery! We recommend you coordinate with the winery before doing so!

Chrysalis Vineyard. Open daily 10:00 a.m. - 5:00 p.m.; closed Thanksgiving, Christmas and New Year's Day. (540) 687-8222; Toll Free (800) 235-8804. www.chrysaliswine.com

Swendenburg Estate Vineyard. Open daily 10:00 a.m. - 4:00 p.m. (540) 687-5219. www.swedenburgwines.com

Delaplane Cellars. Open Thursday - Monday 11:00 a.m. - 5:00 p.m.; Friday until 7:00 p.m. (540) 592-7210. www.delaplanecellars.com

Philip Carter Winery of Virginia. Open daily April - November 11:00 a.m. - 6:00 p.m.; December - March Thursday - Monday 11:00 a.m. - 6:00 p.m. (540) 364-1203. www.pcwinery.com

Piedmont Vineyards & Winery. Open daily April - October 11:00 a.m. - 6:00 p.m.; November - March 11:00 a.m. - 5:00 p.m. (540) 687-5528. www.piedmontwines.com

Three Fox Vineyards. Open Friday - Sunday 12:00 p.m. - 6:00 p.m. or by appointment from April 21st - December 17th. (540) 364-6073. www.threefoxvineyards.com

Naked Mountain Winery & Vineyards. Open daily 11:00 a.m. - 5:00 p.m. Closed Thanksgiving; December 24th - 26th & 31st and New Year's Day. (540) 364-1609. www.nakedmtnwinery.com

Barrel Oak Winery. Open Sunday - Thursday 11:00 a.m. - 6:00 p.m.; Friday 11:00 a.m. - 9:00 p.m.; Saturday 11:00 a.m. - 6:00 p.m. (540) 364-6402. www.barreloak.com

Miracle Valley Vineyard. Open Thursday - Monday 11:00 a.m. - 5:00 p.m. (540) 364-0228. www.miraclevalleyvineyard.com

Vintage Ridge Vineyard. Open Friday - Sunday 11:00 a.m. - 5:00 p.m. from April to early December. (540) 364-3371. www.vintageridgewine.com

Sky Meadows State Park. Open daily 8:00 a.m. - dusk. Hiking, camping, picnic area, Visitor Center, restrooms, parking, scenic points for photographs.

Appalachian Trail. This famous hiking trail running 2,160 miles along the spine of the Appalachian Mountains from Springer Mountain in Georgia to Mount Katahdin in Maine runs within a 1/4 mile of this route at two locations. The first is as you turn off Hwy 7 West onto Blueridge Mountain Rd (SR 601) and the second is as you exit Blueridge Mountain Rd onto Hwy 50 East. The Appalachian Trail runs along the lower western shoulders of the ridgeline as you ride south on Blueridge Mountain Rd.

Crooked Run Valley is joy to ride!

Delaplane Cellars is a nice reward after a ride!

5

Burwell-Morgan Mill

How to Get There (where to park)

To get to the Burwell-Morgan Mill parking area take Exit 23 off of I-66 and get on Hwy 17 North. Take a Left onto Hwy 50 West/17 North. Just over six miles after getting onto Hwy 50 West, take a Right onto Hwy 255 North. Go 1/2 mile and take a Left at the Stop sign. The Burwell-Morgan Mill is 0.1 mile on your left. There is parking directly across the street from the Locke Modern Country Store. From Winchester, take Hwy 50 East/17 South to Hwy 255 North.

Lay o' the Land

This relative short and thoroughly enjoyable ride has an either/or characteristic. Either you are riding along relatively flat, open roads surrounded by large fenced pastures; or you are riding along narrow, winding roads almost grown over by trees beside the Shenandoah River or Spout Run. There is one major descent on this ride - just past the 12th mile - as you drop down to the low water bridge to cross the Shenandoah River. There are only two climbs requiring anything more than a quick jump out of the saddle. One occurs at the 16th mile and the other occurs just before mile 26 as you climb away from Spout Run. The ride is short but there are ample opportunities to pick up food and drink along the way. This ride is easy and oftentimes we do this loop twice - taking a break to tour the mill or relax on the porch of the Locke Modern Country Store before taking a second loop. Except for the section on Howellsville Rd running beside the Shenandoah River, practically this entire ride is on scenic Virginia Byways.

Ride Description

We begin this enjoyable ride by going Right out of the Burwell-Morgan Mill parking lot onto Millwood Rd for a short distance and veering Right onto Hwy 255 (SR 723). Go straight at the Stop sign (use caution crossing Hwy 50/17) onto Red Gate Rd - a Virginia Byway. Take a Right onto Nelson Rd (SR 626) and very shortly you will pass the entrance to historic Long Branch - keep riding and come back to visit after the ride! Take a Right onto Berry's Ferry Rd (SR 628) at 2.2 miles and be careful of the angled RR crossing at mile 4.2. Turn Left onto White Post Rd (SR 658) in the quaint village of White Post.

The namesake White Post in the village of White Post

White Post is home of the spectacular L'Auberge Provencale Bed and Breakfast featuring its Country Inn and Fine Dining. Keep riding! There is another railroad crossing at about mile 6.5 where the road becomes Sugar Hill Rd. This section is wide open with long stretches of relatively flat roadway. You can either really crank up the speed or slow down to enjoy the scenery! Be careful not to miss the Left turn onto Bowling Green Rd (SR 683). There is a small sign for the Bowling

Green Country Club at this turn. There is an opportunity for a rest-room break at mile 10.3 at the golf course clubhouse as well as a chance to pick up something to drink. Just after mile 11 take a Left onto Fairground Rd (SR 661) and then a Right at the Stop sign onto Milldale Rd (SR 624). Milldale Rd carries you across a rough, concrete low water bridge across the Shenandoah River - enjoy the over half-mile downhill to the bridge!

Kevin on the Milldale Rd low water bridge

Shortly after crossing the bridge take a Left onto Howellsville Rd (SR 643) which you stay on for a lazy nine mile ride beside the river. This is an enjoyable ride, even during the heat of the summer as a long portion of the ride is overhung by trees. At mile 16.5 the Shenandoah Farms Grocery provides a stop for a drink, snack or restroom break. Follow Howellsville Rd to the Left at this intersection and be mindful of vehicles entering the road from the right. Three miles beyond Shenandoah Farms Grocery there is a Country Store and Deli on the left - the last opportunity to pick-up food or drink until the end of the ride. Again use caution crossing Hwy 50/17 and in riding almost one mile on Hwy 50/17. Turn Right onto Millwood Rd (SR 723) and then take another Right onto Tilthammer Mill Rd (SR 621) - yet another Virginia Byway! Tilthammer Mill Rd carries you along Spout Run before veering Left onto Clay Hill Rd (SR 651) and its half-mile climb away from Spout Run. You pass horse riding trails on both sides of the road as you ride to the Stop sign and Left turn onto Bishop Mead Rd (Hwy 255) for the short run into Millwood and back to the Burwell-Morgan Mill parking lot.

*Locke Modern Country Store -
parking across the street*

*Alice, Bob Marsh, Kevin & Carol Gardner
with a new friend, Gil
enjoying a lunch stop during Bike Virginia 2010*

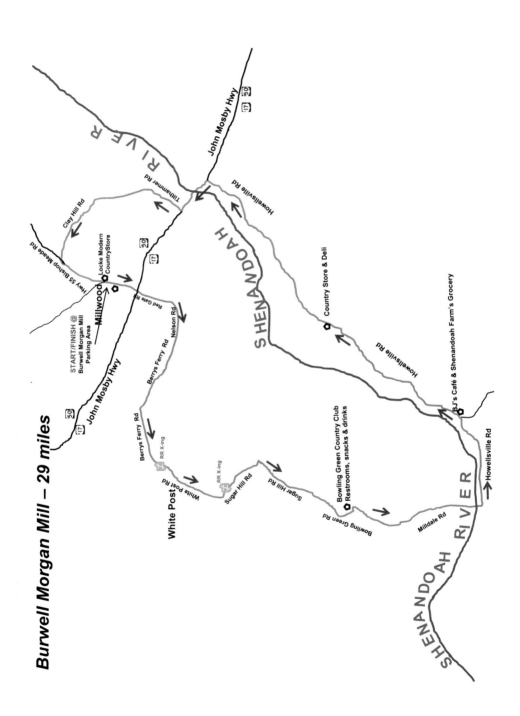

Burwell Morgan Mill – 29 miles

RIVER

John Mosby Hwy
17 50

Clay Hill Rd

Tillhammer Rd

Howellsville Rd

Hwy 55 Bishop Meade Rd

Locke Modern CountryStore

50
17

SHENANDOAH

Country Store & Deli

Millwood

START/FINISH @ Burwell Morgan Mill Parking Area

Red Gate Rd

Nelson Rd

BJ's Café & Shenandoah Farm's Grocery

John Mosby Hwy

Berrys Ferry Rd

Howellsville Rd

50
17

Berrys Ferry Rd

RR X-ing

White Post Rd

RR X-ing

Sugar Hill Rd

Sugar Hill Rd

Bowling Green Country Club
Restrooms, snacks & drinks

Howellsville Rd

White Post

Bowling Green Rd

Milldale Rd

SHENANDOAH RIVER

~ Refer to page 10 for Ride Map Color Codes ~

Burwell-Morgan Mill Cue Sheet

	Total	Segment
R out of parking lot on Millwood Rd (Hwy 255/SR 723)		0.1
BR on Hwy 255 **VBW**	0.1	0.6
SA Hwy 50/17 @ **SS** on Red Gate Rd (SR 624) **VBW**	0.7	0.6
R on Nelson Rd (SR 626) **VBW**	1.3	0.9
R on Berry's Ferry Rd (SR 628) **VBW**	2.2	2.0
RR (angled)	4.2	0.5
L on White Post Rd (SR 658) **VBW**	4.7	1.8
RR; **BEC** Sugar Hill Rd (SR 658) **VBW**	6.5	3.2
L on Bowling Green Rd (SR 683)	9.7	0.6
Bowling Green Country Club Golf Pro Shop on left (restrooms & soft drinks/snacks available in pro shop)	10.3	0.8
L on Fairground Rd (SR 611)	11.1	0.4
R on Milldale Rd (SR 624)	11.5	1.3
Low water bridge across the Shenandoah River	12.8	0.3
L on Howellsville Rd (SR 643)	13.1	3.4
BL on Howellsville Rd (**BEC** SR 638); Shenandoah Farm's Grocery @ intersection	16.5	2.9
Jim's Country Store and Deli on left	19.4	3.1
L on Hwy 50/17 West; **TRAFFIC**	22.5	0.9
R on Millwood Rd (SR 723)	23.4	0.1
R on Tilthammer Mill Rd (SR 621) **VBW**	23.5	2.1
BL on Clay Hill Rd (SR 651) **VBW**	25.6	1.4
L @ **SS** on Bishop Meade Rd (Hwy 255) **VBW**	27.0	1.4
L @ **SS** on Hwy 255/SR 723; Burwell-Morgan Mill parking lot is immediately on right after making the turn	28.4	

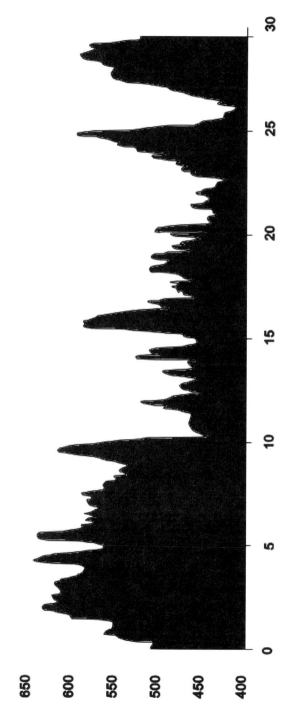

Burwell-Morgan Mill Elevation Profile
Start: 510 ft   Low: 410 ft   High: 642 ft
Total Gain: 1,869 ft   Distance: 29 mi
Average Elevation Gain: 64 ft/mile

Places to Eat

Yet another reason we enjoy this ride are the awesome deli sandwiches offered in the Locke Modern Country Store situated across the street from the Burwell-Morgan Mill. As noted in the ride description, there are several opportunities for snacks and deli sandwiches along the route and even the opportunity for a luxury meal at the L'Auberge Provencale! Another option is to drive back to Middleburg and enjoy one of the delightful opportunities to eat there.

Local Bike Shops

There are no bike shops along this ride. Ensure your bike is properly tuned before going on this ride and ensure the ride group carries the proper equipment for typical roadside repair.

Local Attractions

Burwell-Morgan Mill. Open from May - Thanksgiving. Tours, restrooms, and picnic area. www.clarkehistory.org/themill.htm

Historic Long Branch. Historic old mansion and grounds. Public events throughout the year. www.historiclongbranch.com

L'Auberge Provencale Bed and Breakfast. Located in White Post. Luxurious country inn and fine dining. www.laubergeprovencale.com/rooms.html

The State Arboretum of Virginia. Located in Boyce at the University of Virginia's Blandy Experimental Farm research facility. www.virginia.edu/blandy

Veramar Vineyard. Located at 905 Quarry Rd, Berryville, VA 22611. (540) 955-5510. www.info@veramar.com

6

Middletown

How to Get There (where to park)

Larrick's Tavern located in the Wayside Inn, makes for a terrific post-ride stop to relax and enjoy something to eat and drink!"

Getting to Middletown from the D.C. Beltway is easy. Take I-66 West to I-81 North towards Winchester. Take Exit 2 and go Left on SR 627 Reliance Road - you cross over I-81 - until you get to Hwy 11. Take a Left onto Hwy 11 South for about 1/2-mile and take a Right onto 2nd St. Go straight across Senseny Ave and park in the Middletown Community Park parking lot which also has restroom facilities.

If you are traveling from points south, just get on I-81 North to Exit 2 and follow the directions above. If you are traveling from points north, just get on I-81 South to Exit 2 and follow the directions above.

Lay o' the Land

Like just about every other area in the Shenandoah Valley, the terrain around Middletown is terrific for road biking. This ride is generally bounded by I-81 to the east, Hwy 50 to the north, Great North Mountain to the west, and then Hwy 55 to the south. The ride is characterized by rolling farmland, orchards and pastures nearer Winchester as you pedal north and then transforming into rougher, forested terrain, as you turn south along Wardensville Grade Road. Main street Middletown is not very big but is a friendly, welcoming small town in which to grab a bite to eat; rest, and visit after your ride.

Ride Description

This is a challenging ride but well worth the effort due to the beautiful and varied terrain. Exiting Middletown, you head west to Middle Rd for the run north towards Winchester to Cedar Creek Grade. The terrain from Middletown to Cedar Creek Grade is rolling farmland. Cedar Creek Grade takes you around the northern shoulder of Little North Mountain. This terrain is rolling farmland with orchards and pastures spread throughout - a generally easy ride. The homes you pass are an interesting mixture of older homesteads, new construction and "McMansions." After rounding Little North Mountain's shoulder, Wardensville Grade takes you through generally forested terrain in a southwesterly direction between Little North Mountain to the east and Great North Mountain to the west. Wardensville Grade is around 14 miles of challenging riding with both longer steady climbs and the occasionally short steep climb guaranteed to get your out of your saddle!

As you turn onto Hwy 55 East (alternately named either John Marshall Highway or Wardensville Pike), you will find the Corners Bar & Grill. If the Corners Bar & Grill is not open, your first opportunity for drinks and snacks is at the Garden Supermarket on your left at mile 36.7. The first opportunity for a bathroom, - not counting the trees and bushes lining the road - is at mile 40.5 at the Shell station & Food Mart on the left. Shortly after the Food Mart, you get on Clary Rd, which takes you to Hwy 11 North and into Middletown.

Entrance to Belle Grove Plantation

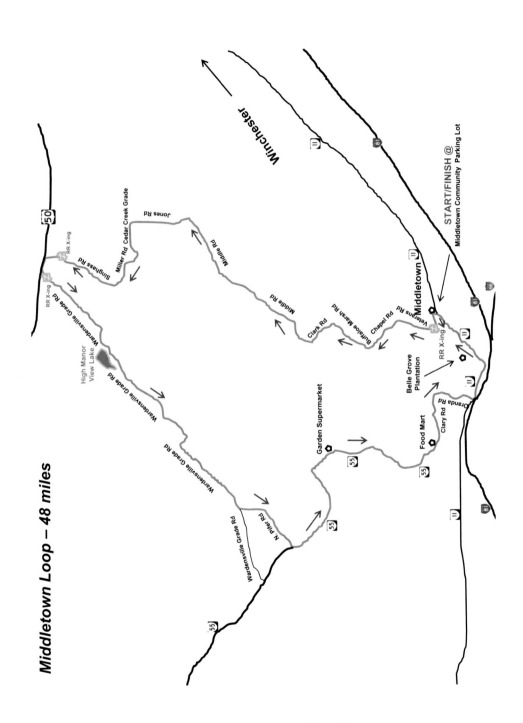

Middletown Loop – 48 miles

~ *Refer to page 10 for Ride Map Color Codes* ~

Middletown Loop Cue Sheet

	Total	Segment
R on Senseny Ave out of parking lot		0.3
R @ **SS** on 5th St (SR 625; **BEC** Veterans Rd)	0.3	0.5
RR; **S** on Veterans Rd 100 meters after **RR**	0.8	0.5
BEC gravel rd	1.3	0.5
L @ **SS** on Chapel Rd (SR 627)	1.8	1.8
R on Buffalo Marsh Rd (SR 759) - easy to miss!	3.6	1.3
L @ **SS** on Clark Rd (SR 638)	4.9	1.3
R on Middle Rd (SR 628)	6.2	5.6
L on Jones Rd (SR 621)	11.8	1.9
L @ **SS** on Cedar Grade Rd (SR 622)	13.7	1.5
Sharp R in Opequon on Miller Rd (SR 620)	15.2	1.3
R to stay on SR 620; **BEC** Singhass Rd	16.5	2.1
RR; **L** @ **YS** (on hill!) on Round Hill Rd (SR 803)	18.6	0.4
L on Hwy 50 West - **TRAFFIC**	19.0	0.2
L on Wardensville Grade Rd (SR 608); then **RR**	19.2	10.2
BL @ **SS TRO** Wardensville Grade Rd	29.4	0.7
BL on N. Pifer Rd @ Mountain View United Methodist Church sign	30.1	2.6
L @ **SS** on Hwy 55 East (Wardensville Pike)	32.7	5.6
Woodbine Farm Market on right	38.3	2.5
L on Clary Rd	40.8	1.7
R @ **SS** on Oranda Rd (SR 629)	42.5	1.0
RR	43.5	1.2
L @ **SS** on Hwy 11 North	44.7	3.3
L on 2nd St	48.0	0.1
S @ **SS** across Senseny Ave to parking lot	48.1	

~ Refer to page 9 for Cue Sheet Symbology ~

Middletown Loop Elevation Profile

Start: 693 ft   Low: 530 ft   High: 1,127 ft

Total Gain: 3,180 ft   Distance: 48 mi

Average Elevation Gain: 66 ft/mile

Places to Eat

Middletown is a small town with a couple of terrific places to eat after a challenging ride - The Irish Isle Restaurant & Pub, located at 7843 Main Street, Middletown, VA 22645. Open from 4:00 p.m. daily (noon Saturday & Sunday). Larrick's Tavern is located within the Wayside Inn and is open from 11:30 a.m. - 9:00 p.m. Larrick's Tavern was built in 1742 and has both lunch and dinner menus featuring traditional Virginia dishes. Larrick's also serves a wide variety of domestic and imported wines and beers.

Irish Isle Restaurant & Pub

Local Bike Shops

There are no bike shops in Middletown and there are no bike shops along this route so you will need to ensure your bike is prepared for a challenging ride before you arrive in Middletown. The three closest bike shops are in Winchester.

Element Sports located at 2184 South Pleasant Valley Rd is open 9:00 a.m. - 7:00 p.m. Monday - Friday; 9:00 a.m. - 6:00 p.m. Saturday and 12:00 p.m. - 5:00 p.m. Sunday. Phone: (540) 662-5744.

Blue Ridge Schwinn located at 2228G Papermill Rd is open 10:00 a.m. - 6:00 p.m. Monday - Friday; 10:00 a.m. - 5:00 p.m. Saturday; closed Sunday. Phone: (540) 662-1510.

Black Bar Bicycles, LLC located at 3113 Valley Ave is open 10:00 a.m. - 7:00 p.m. Monday - Friday; 10:00 a.m. - 4:00 p.m. Saturday; closed Sunday for riding. Phone: (540) 535-0188.

Local Attractions

Middletown has several local attractions and others within a short drive. Some of the more popular attractions include:

The Wayside Theatre, located at 7853 Main St, Middletown, VA 22645 is a local community theatre with professional productions. (540) 869-1776. www.waysidetheatre.org

Wayside Inn

The Wayside Inn, located at 7783 Main St, Middletown, VA 22645 has been operating since 1797 providing comfortable rooms and outstanding food to weary travelers. Call (540) 869-1797 for reservations. www.alongthewayside.com

Belle Grove Plantation located in one mile south of Middletown, VA on Hwy 11. www.bellegrove.org

Vino Curioso is a Boutique Winery located at 1334 Perry Road, Winchester, VA 22602. (703) 447-0648. The tasting room is open weekends from 11:00 a.m. to 5:00 p.m. Please call ahead to make an appointment. www.vinocurioso.com

North Mountain Vineyard and Winery is located at 4374 Swartz Rd, Maurertown, VA 22644. Open Wednesday-Sunday from 11:00 a.m. to 5:00 p.m. (540) 436-9463. www.northmountainvineyard.com

*North Mountain Vineyard and Winery
is always a terrific place to stop.*

Carolina Tailwinds Bicycling Vacations van and trailer

7

Strasburg

How to Get There (where to park)

The Hotel Strasburg is a local institution

Getting to Strasburg from the D.C. Beltway is simple. Take I-66 West to I-81 South towards Winchester. Take Exit 298 and go Left on Hwy 11 South. Follow Hwy 11 South for about two miles just past the intersection of Hwy 11 and Hwy 55. Take a Left at the light onto Hwy 55 East and one block later you can find parking on the right between Jalisco Authentic Mexican Restaurant and Subway. Subway has restroom facilities for your final pre-ride restroom break.

If you are traveling from points south, just get on I-81 North to Exit 296 and go Right onto Hwy 55 East for a mile and a half when you run into Hwy 11 South. Go right on Hwy 11 South and then Left at the next light onto Hwy 55 East.

If you are traveling from points north, just get on I-81 South to Exit 298 and follow the directions above.

Lay o' the Land

Like other areas in the Shenandoah Valley, the terrain around Strasburg is terrific for road biking. The Fort Valley ride is generally bounded by Little North Mountain to the west, I-81 running through the middle and then riding east through Edinburg Gap into Fort Valley and then north through Fort Valley to Hwy 55 and back into Strasburg. The ride is characterized by rolling farmland and pastures as you ride south along Back Road and east towards Edinburg Gap; then transforming into rougher, forested terrain, as you climb through Edinburg Gap and north the length of Fort Valley.

The Cedar Creek Battlefield ride is also bounded by Little North Mountain to the West as you ride north, and then by I-81 to the East as you turn and ride back South through Middletown and the Cedar Creek Battlefield on Hwy 11 South. This ride takes you into some of the orchard country west of I-81 with rolling hills and farmland and pastures as you pedal north. There are some incredible vistas on this ride as you look south "up" the Shenandoah Valley. You can clearly see why Signal Knob was such an important piece of terrain during the Civil War.

Ride Descriptions

Fort Valley Loop

Walkers Cash Store has fresh deli
sandwiches and cold drinks!

This is a fun ride with one climb through Edinburg Gap and then generally descending as your ride north through Fort Valley. Exiting Strasburg, you head south and then west to Back Rd for the run south towards Edinburg. There is a Handy Mart and the M&R Mart on your right as you leave Strasburg so there is a final opportunity to fill the water bottles and grab a snack for the ride. The ride from Hwy 11 to Back Rd generally climbs the entire way. Back Rd is a series of rolling hills as you ride south until the turn onto St. Luke Rd. At mile 8.7 is the turn to North Mountain Vineyard and Winery (a great post-ride stop! - tell John we said hello!). There are large farms and varied houses along both sides of Back Rd. Walkers Cash Store is on the right as you turn Left onto St. Luke Rd. Heading east on St. Luke Rd you are looking directly at Powell Mountain. From this point until you cross the North Fork of the Shenandoah River, the ride is basically downhill and then you begin the climb across Edinburg Gap to Kings Crossing. When you bear Left onto Readus Rd you are riding directly towards Edinburg Gap. At mile 23.8 is the turn to Shenandoah Vineyards. Edinburg is a small town with several opportunities to stop for drinks and a bathroom break. Exiting Edinburg you immediately cross North Fork of the Shenandoah River and begin your climb to Edinburg Gap. The crest of the gap is at mile 28.5 followed by a thrilling downhill of two miles to Kings Crossing. The ride north through Fort Valley is one of smaller farms generally becoming more forested as you get closer to exiting Fort Valley to the north. Fort Valley Country Store is on the left @ mile 37.2 and the Fort Valley Museum is @ mile 38.7. The road closely follows Passage Creek the last few miles out of the valley. You may even want to the opportunity to stop and take a quick dip in the cool water! Once you make the Left turn onto Hwy 55 West the road is generally flat back into Strasburg with a slight dip and climb as you cross over the North Fork of the Shenandoah River. Use caution of this stretch of road as the speed limit is 55 mph and there is not a large shoulder on the road.

Cedar Creek Battlefield

Cedar Creek Battlefield - south of Middletown

This is one of the shorter rides in the book but is one of the most enjoyable. You get terrific views of the northern Shenandoah Valley; there are some excellent places to take breaks and Jalisco's is at the end of the ride! The first six miles are exactly the same as the Fort Valley ride. You exit Strasburg on Hwy 11 South and then make the same climb west across I-81 to Back Rd. However, on this ride you make a Right turn onto Back Rd and experience the same longer rolling hills as you pedal north into the apple orchard country after crossing Hwy 55. The Woodbine Farm Market is on the left at mile 12.7. They have clean restrooms, drinks and fresh, home-baked goodies - making for a terrific SAG stop. During the summer months there is an ice cream stand and on weekends there is a fresh BBQ stand at the Woodbine Farm Market. The ride becomes generally less hilly after crossing Cedar Creek on Middle Rd. The terrain is more open with orchards on both sides of the road until the turn onto Marlboro Rd. You are on Marlboro Rd for not quite a mile before turning Right onto Hites Rd. The ride along Hites Rd is open farmland until you get to Chapel Rd and then into Middletown. As you exit Middletown, the Family Country Market is on the right. They have a terrific deli section as well as hot food and drinks. Just past the Family Country Market on Hwy 11 South, you ride through the main portion of the Cedar Creek Battlefield and can see the Belle Grove Plantation Manor House across the fields to your right. The Cedar Creek Battlefield Headquarters is on the left at mile 25, and just 0.2 mile before the Right turn to the Belle Grove Manor House. The Belle Grove Manor House is open to visitors for guided tours daily April-December. About one mile after crossing I-81, you start down the hill into Strasburg and the end of the ride.

The Woodbine Farm Market is a great stop!

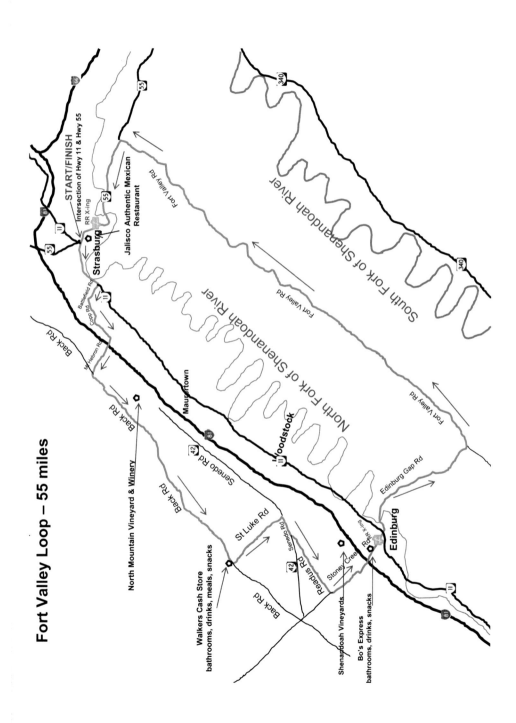

Fort Valley Loop – 55 miles

START/FINISH
Intersection of Hwy 11 & Hwy 55

RR X-ing

Strasburg

Jalisco Authentic Mexican Restaurant

Fort Valley Rd

Battlefield Rd

Copp Rd

Mt Hebron Rd

Back Rd

Back Rd

North Mountain Vineyard & Winery

Back Rd

Mauertown

Woodstock

North Fork of Shenandoah River

Fort Valley Rd

South Fork of Shenandoah River

Edinburg Gap Rd

Fort Valley Rd

Senedo Rd

St Luke Rd

Walkers Cash Store
bathrooms, drinks, meals, snacks

Back Rd

Reedys Rd

Senedo Rd

Stoney Creek

Shenandoah Vineyards

Bo's Express
bathrooms, drinks, snacks

RR X-ing

Edinburg

~ Refer to page 10 for Ride Map Color Codes ~

Fort Valley Loop Cue Sheet

	Total	Segment
Start at the intersection of Hwy 11/Hwy 55; go South on Hwy 11 (Old Valley Pike)		1.8
R on SR 601 (Battlefield Rd)	1.8	0.7
BL on SR 757 (Copp Rd)	2.5	1.9
R @ **SS** @ **T-intersection** on SR 646 (Mt. Hebron Rd)	4.4	1.9
L @ **SS** on SR 623 (Back Rd)	6.3	8.9
L on SR 605 (St Luke Rd); **Walkers Cash Store** on corner on right	15.2	2.4
R @ **SS TRO** SR 605 (St Luke Rd)	17.6	0.5
R @ **SS** on Hwy 42 (Senedo Rd)	18.1	1.0
BL on SR 642 (Readus Rd)	19.1	1.7
S @ **4WS TRO** SR 642 (Readus Rd)	20.8	0.6
L @ **SS** on SR 675 (Stoney Creek Rd)	21.4	2.6
RR	24.0	0.2
L @ **SS** on Hwy 11 North	24.2	0.6
R on SR 675 (Edinburg Gap Rd)	24.8	5.6
L @ **SS** on SR 678 (Ft Valley Rd)	30.4	19.2
L @ **SS** on Hwy 55 West (Strasburg Rd)	49.6	4.7
RR	54.3	0.2
End @ Hwy 11/Hwy 55 Intersection	54.5	

~ *Refer to page 9 for Cue Sheet Symbology* ~

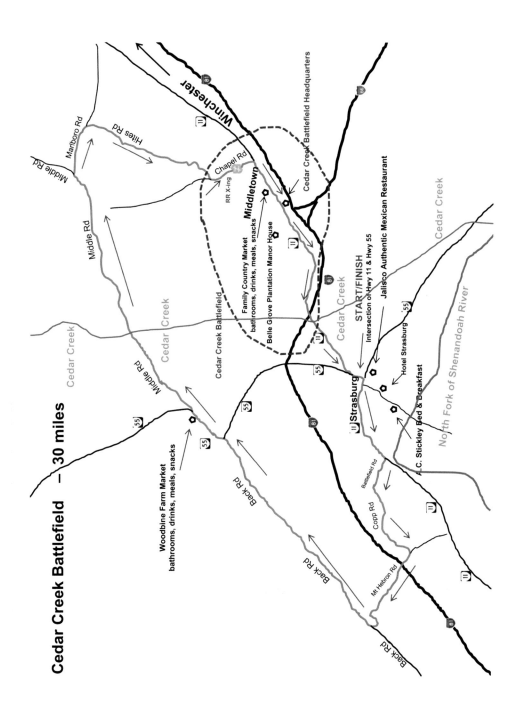

Cedar Creek Battlefield — 30 miles

Cedar Creek Battlefield Cue Sheet

	Total	Segment
Route starts at the intersection of Hwy 11 & Hwy 55; South on Hwy 11 (Old Valley Pike) for		1.8
R on SR 601 (Battlefield Rd)	1.8	0.7
BL on SR 757 (Copp Rd)	2.5	2.0
R @ **SS** on SR 646 (Mt. Hebron Rd)	4.4	1.9
R @ **SS** on SR 623 (Back Rd)	6.3	5.5
L @ **SS** on Hwy 55 West	11.5	1.4
Woodbine Farm Market on left @ 12.7		
BR on SR 628 (Middle Road) @ Lebanon Church	12.9	5.3
R on SR 631 (Marlboro Rd)	18.2	0.9
R on SR 625 (Hites Rd)	19.1	3.5
L on SR 627 (Chapel Rd)	22.6	0.7
2RR	23.3	0.6
R on Hwy 11 South	23.6	5.5
Family Country Market on right @ 24.4		
Optional **R** to go to Belle Grove Manor House @ 25.2		
End @ Hwy 11/Hwy 55 intersection	29.1	

~ Refer to page 9 for Cue Sheet Symbology ~

Fort Valley Loop Elevation Profile

Start: 571 ft   Low: 513 ft   High: 1,657 ft
Total Gain: 2,218 ft   Distance: 55 mi
Average Elevation Gain: 40 ft/mile

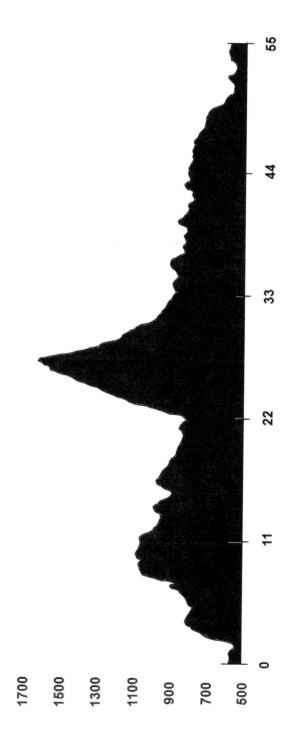

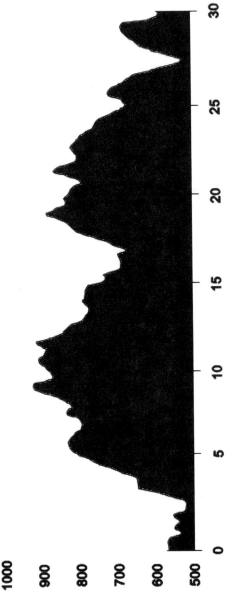

Cedar Creek Battlefield Elevation Profile

Start: 571 ft   Low: 525 ft   High: 932 ft

Total Gain: 2,036 ft   Distance: 30 mi

Average Elevation Gain: 68 ft/mile

Places to Eat

Strasburg is a small town with several nice places to eat after a challenging ride. Our favorite is Jalisco Authentic Mexican Restaurant - one reason we normally park in the lot beside the restaurant. If you are in a hurry, the Subway is an option as well. Hotel Strasburg is another excellent option if you have a little more time. Cristina's Café is a local café with fresh sandwiches and plenty of local flavor.

Jalisco's is our favorite post-ride eatery in Strasburg

Local Bike Shops

There are no bike shops in Strasburg and there are no bike shops along this route so you will need to ensure your bike is prepared to ride before you arrive in Strasburg.

Local Attractions

Strasburg has several local attractions and others within a short drive. Some of the more popular attractions include:

The Strasburg Museum, located at 440 East King St is open May 1 to October 31 10:00 a.m. until 4:00 p.m. daily. (540) 465-3175.

The Great Strasburg Emporium, located at 160 North Massanutten St is an incredible antique destination. Don't go unless you have plenty of time to look around! Open 10:00 a.m. - 5:00 p.m. daily; 10:00 a.m. - 6:00 p.m. Friday & Saturday. (540) 465-3711.

Buggy B's, located at 238 East King St offers unique gifts and fresh flower arrangements as well as locally designed and manufactured furniture. 540-465-2707. www.buggybs.com

The Hotel Strasburg, located at 213 South Holliday St, Strasburg, VA 22657 is a local landmark known for charming southern hospitality and good food. (800) 348-8327. www.hotelstrasburg.com

Chris Miller tends bar in The Hotel Strasburg's Depot Lounge

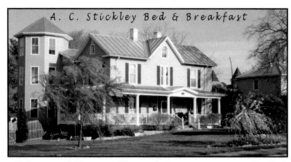

John and Donna Huntsberger are wonderful hosts at the A.C. Stickley Bed and Breakfast

The A.C. Stickley Bed and Breakfast, located at 384 South Holliday Street, Strasburg, VA 22657 is a great place to spend the weekend and relax in one of its whirlpool tubs after a ride! (540) 335-6287. www.acstickleybandb.com

Belle Grove Plantation located in four miles north of Strasburg, VA on Hwy 11. www.bellegrove.org

North Mountain Vineyard and Winery is located at 4374 Swartz Rd, Maurertown, VA 22644. Open Wednesdays-Sundays from 11:00 a.m. to 5:00 p.m. (540) 436-9463. www.northmountainvineyard.com.

Shenandoah Vineyards has excellent wines and is easily accessible at mile 23.8. The hours are March-November 10:00 a.m. - 6:00 p.m. Phone is (540) 984-8699. www.shentel.net/shenvine.

Chester Gap Cellars is one of our favorite wineries. Bernd and Kristi Jung are warm hosts and their wines are awesome! Located, appropriately enough at the Chester Gap in the Blue Ridge mountains, about four miles south of Front Royal on Hwy 522 South (4615 Remount Rd, Front Royal, Virginia 22630). Hours: Fridays 12:00 p.m. - 6 p.m.; Saturdays 11:00 a.m. - 6:00 p.m.; Sundays 12:00 p.m. - 5:00 p.m. Memorial Day and Labor Day 11:00 a.m. - 5:00 p.m. You may also contact Bernd to make an off-hours or private tasting appointment by calling him @ 540-636-8086 or by email @ Bernd@ChesterGapCellars.com

Rappahannock Cellars. Open daily all year 10:30 a.m. - 5:00 p.m. Sat 10:30 a.m. - 6:00 p.m. (540) 635-9398. www.rappahannockcellars.com

Desert Rose Ranch and Winery is an experience! Located at 13726 Hume Rd, Hume, Virginia 22639. House: Thursday-Monday 1:00 p.m. - 6:00 p.m. 540-635-3200. www.desertrosewinery.com

Glen Manor Vineyards makes terrific wines! Jeff only makes quality wines and releases no wine unless it meets his exacting standard. Address is 2244 Browntown Rd, Front Royal, Virginia 22630. Hours: April-November Wednesday - Saturday 11:00 a.m. - 5:00 p.m., Sundays 12:00 p.m. - 5:00 p.m.; December-March Fridays and Saturdays 11:00 a.m. - 5:00 p.m., Sundays 12:00 p.m. - 5:00 p.m. Closed Thanksgiving Day, Christmas Day through New Year's Day, and Easter Sunday. 540- 635-6324. www.glenmanorvineyards.com

8

Winchester Loop

How to Get There (where to park)

Getting to Winchester from the D.C. Beltway is easy. Take I-66 West to I-81 North. Take Exit 313 and as you cross over I-81 bear Left onto East Jubal Early Drive and then Left into the Apple Blossom Mall parking lot. There are many fast food restaurants where you can make a final bathroom break before beginning your ride. We recommend parking near Sears as that parking area allows the most direct access to the route. If traveling from the north or south, just take I-81 to Exit 313 and follow the above directions.

Lay o' the Land

The Winchester area is terrific for road biking as Winchester has plenty of places to eat before and after the rides as well as plenty of public bathrooms. The Winchester terrain is characterized by rolling farmland, orchards and pastures nearer the city and then transforming into rougher, forested terrain, as you get further away from the city. Downtown Winchester is a pleasant place

Orchards - a typical sight on his ride

to rest and visit after your ride - sit back and enjoy the town! Two annual events you will want to catch are the Shenandoah Apple Blossom Festival in early May each year and the Peach Festival in mid-August each year.

Ride Description

Unless you decide to ride a Century ride on Skyline Drive, this is the longest and the most challenging ride in the book. Broken up into distinct sections of topography this ride has something for everyone. The first 25 miles are rolling hills of the northern piedmont. The next

A curious emu walks towards the fence along Back Mountain Rd while the horse walks away - you never know what you will see on the rides!

15 miles are characterized by long climbs, steep climbs and the down hills that come after climbs. The road twists and turns through the mountains of extreme northern Virginia until you cross over Hwy 522. The next almost 10 miles are easy riding south along the valley between Great North Mountain to the West and Little North Mountain to the East. The route then turns east and gets challenging again as you ride over Little North Mountain back to Cedar Creek Grade for the final six+ miles back into Winchester to the Apple Blossom Mall parking lot.

Though challenging, this ride contains views of the beautiful northern Virginia countryside characteristic of all rides in this book. Beginning with the horse farms along Senseny Rd to the rural farms and orchards north of Winchester; you know you are in a special place for bikes. Mountain farms and rustic roadways characterize the ride once you get on Green Spring Road at mile 25. Use caution as wildlife abounds and if some of it bounds in front of you on the road, you will need to react quickly to avoid a collision! The ride south along North and South Hayfield Roads is spectacular as you spin through the valley between Great North Mountain and Little North Mountain. Crossing East over Little North Mountain to Cedar Creek Grade takes you through some more mountainous terrain but it is less challenging than the previous section. Finally, the ride along Cedar Creek Grade is easy rolling hills back into Winchester.

Another thing we like about this ride is the easy availability of stores along the way to grab food and drink. There is a Handy Mart and Deli at an Exxon station at mile 2.8 and the County Park Plaza (with a pizza joint!) at mile 3.2. The Triple J Convenience Store is located at the intersection of Triple J Rd and Route 7 (mile 9.8). There is a CITGO Station at the intersection of Route 11 and Hopewell Rd (mile 20.2). The NB Market is on the right as you cross Hwy 50 at mile 43.4. At mile 47.1 on Back Mountain Rd is Tom's Market and as you enter Winchester after mile 61, there are many stores.

Owner Davy DeHaven is building a smoker in the Spring of 2012 so he can serve BBQ at his NB Market. Very clean bathrooms as well!

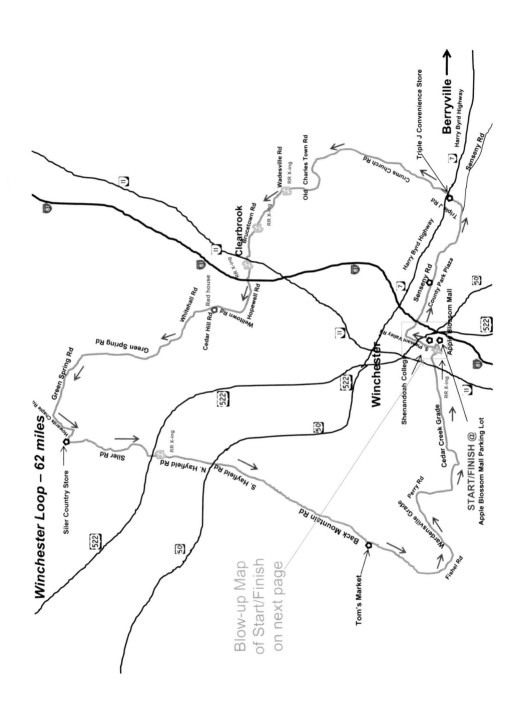

Winchester Loop – 62 miles

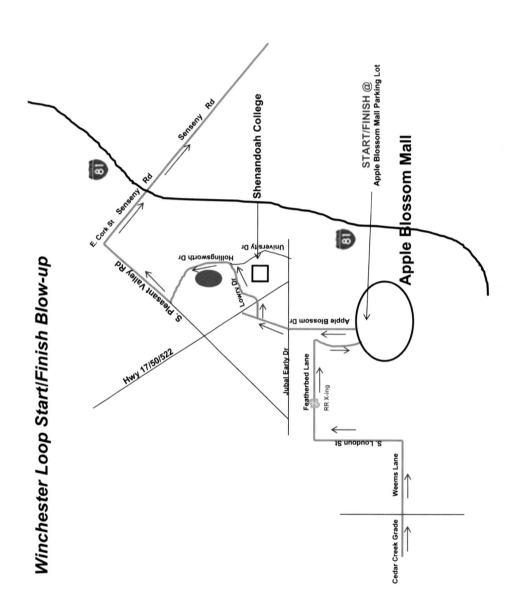

Winchester Loop Start/Finish Blow-up

Winchester Loop Cue Sheet

	Total	Segment
Exit Apple Blossom Mall parking lot onto Apple Blossom Drive		0.1
S @ **TL** across Jubal Early Dr	0.1	0.2
R @ **TL** on Pleasant Valley Rd	0.3	0.7
R @ **TL** on Cork St	1.2	0.5
Cross over I-81; **BEC** Senseny Rd (SR 657)	1.7	5.7
L on Triple J Rd (SR 632)	7.4	2.3
SA Hwy 7 onto Crums Church Rd (SR 632); **7-11 Store** on corner	9.7	4.1
L on Old Charles Town Rd (SR 761)	13.8	1.4
R on Wadesville Rd (SR 661)	15.2	1.6
RR (ROUGH)	16.8	0.1
L @ **SS** on Swimley Rd (SR 672)	16.9	0.1
L @ **SS** (after crossing 1-lane bridge) on Brucetown Rd (SR 672)	17.0	2.8
RR (ANGLED)	19.8	0.4
L @ **SS** on Hwy 11 south; **QR** on Hopewell Rd (SR 672); **CITGO Station** and market on corner; then **RR**	20.2	0.2
Cross over I-81	20.4	1.8
R @ **SS** on Welltown Rd (SR 661)	22.2	1.0
L on Cedar Hill Rd (SR 671); easy to miss; turn 100 yards after *Red* house on left	23.2	1.1
BEC Whitehall Rd (SR 671)	24.3	0.6
S @ **4WS** on Green Spring Rd	24.9	7.1

(continued on back)

~ Refer to page 9 for Cue Sheet Symbology ~

	Total	Segment
BL on Howards Chapel Rd (SR 690)	32.0	1.7
BL on Siler Rd (SR 600)	33.7	5.8
SA Hwy 522 @ **SS**	39.5	0.2
RR (ANGLED)	39.7	0.1
L @ **SS** on Gainesboro Rd (SR 600)	39.8	0.2
R on North Hayfield Rd (SR 600)	40.0	3.4
SA Hwy 50 @ **SS**; **BEC** South Hayfield Rd (SR 600); **NB Market** on the corner	43.4	2.0
R @ **SS** on Back Mountain Rd (SR 600)	45.4	1.7
Tom's Market on right	47.1	2.0
L on Fishel Rd (SR 612); easy to miss	49.1	1.5
L @ **SS** on Wardensville Grade Rd (SR 608); caution - **SS** is on a steep incline!	50.6	3.0
R on Perry Rd (SR 619)	53.6	3.0
L @ **SS** on Cedar Creek Grade	56.6	3.9
Enter Winchester - **Congestion**	60.5	0.5
SA Hwy 11 @ **TL** onto Weems Lane	61.0	0.6
L @ **TL** on South Loudoun St	61.6	0.3
R @ **TL** on Featherbed Lane	61.9	0.1
RR	62.0	0.2
S @ **TL**	62.2	0.1
R towards Apple Blossom Mall parking lot	62.3	0.1
Apple Blossom Mall parking lot	62.4	

~ *Refer to page 9 for Cue Sheet Symbology* ~

Winchester Loop Elevation Profile

Start: 668 ft   Low: 472 ft   High: 1,161 ft

Total Gain: 4,136 ft   Distance: 63 mi

Average Elevation Gain: 66 ft/mile

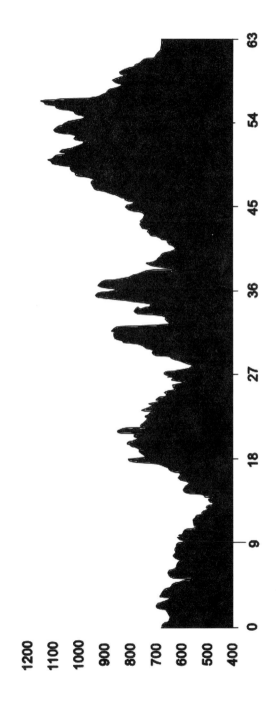

Places to Eat

Winchester is home to Shenandoah University - that means there are enough pizza choices for all discerning cyclists! Winchester has restaurants to fit every palate, price range and time schedule with many places within easy walking distance of the Apple Blossom Mall parking lot.

Local Bike Shops

There are three easily accessible bike shops in Winchester.

Element Sports located at 2184 South Pleasant Valley Rd is open 9:00 a.m. - 7:00 p.m. Monday - Friday; 9:00 a.m. - 6:00 p.m. Saturday and 12:00 p.m. - 5:00 p.m. Sunday. Phone: (540) 662-5744.

Blue Ridge Schwinn located at 2228G Papermill Rd is open 10:00 a.m. - 6:00 p.m. Monday - Friday; 10:00 a.m. - 5:00 p.m. Saturday; closed Sunday. Phone: (540) 662-1510.

Black Bar Bicycles, LLC located at 3113 Valley Ave is open 10:00 a.m. - 7:00 p.m. Monday - Friday; 10:00 a.m. - 4:00 p.m. Saturday; closed Sunday for riding. Phone: (540) 535-0188.

Local Attractions

Winchester has a terrific downtown pedestrian zone on the Loudoun St walking mall with interesting shops, cafés, and restaurants. Within Winchester, some of the more popular attractions include:

The Stonewall Jackson Museum located at 415 North Braddock St.

The Glen Burnie Museum located at 530 Amherst St.

The Shenandoah Valley Discovery Museum located at 54 South Loudoun St.

Road Sign & Tasting Room of Vino Curioso

Vino Curioso is a Boutique Winery located at 1334 Perry Road, Winchester, VA 22602. (703) 447-0648. The tasting room is open weekends from 11:00 a.m. to 5:00 p.m. Please call ahead to make an appointment. www.vinocurioso.com

9

Skyline Drive
Front Royal to Big Meadows

How to Get There (where to park)

From the Washington, D.C. metropolitan area, there are two primary options for accessing Skyline Drive - via the Northern entrance just south of Front Royal or via the Thornton Gap entrance just west of Sperryville. If driving from the I-81 corridor, the best way to get to the Northern entrance of Skyline Drive is by getting onto I-66 East to Exit 6 and then take Hwy 340 South through Front Royal to the entrance. If traveling from the I-81 corridor, the best way to get to the Thornton Gap entrance is by taking Hwy 211 East at Exit 264 in New Market. Stay on Hwy 211 East for approximately 24 miles to the Thornton Gap entrance.

Northern entrance to Skyline Drive. Travel time from the D.C. Beltway to the Front Royal northern entrance to Skyline Drive is approximately 75 minutes. Go west on I-66 for just over 50 miles to Exit 13. Go Left at the bottom of the exit ramp to the first light where you will go Right on Hwy 55 West. After a few miles you will enter Front Royal - the Canoe Capitol of Virginia! Stay on Hwy 55 West through four lights to the "T" intersection with Hwy 340. Go Left on Hwy 340 South for almost 1/2 mile where you will take a Left to the entrance of Skyline Drive. There are big brown Department of the Interior signs all the way from I-66 in case you would rather just follow those signs.

There are parking spaces on the right

Northern Entrance to Shenandoah National Park and Skyline Drive. Park on the side of the road by the sign.

shoulder of the roadway just after the left turn if you want to tackle the climb to Dickey Ridge. For those who would rather not begin with a strenuous five mile climb you can drive to the Dickey Ridge Visitor Center. In addition to a beautiful view you will find plenty of parking, clean restrooms and a water fountain. The Dickey Ridge Visitor Center opens in the Spring and closes in late Fall depending on the weather. The Visitor Center has soft drinks and a small assortment of snacks though you would definitely NOT want to attempt to stock-up on food at the Visitor Center.

Options at the Thornton Gap entrance. There is parking just across the bridge over Hwy 211

Thornton Gap entrance to Skyline Drive. Travel time from the Beltway to the Thornton Gap entrance is also 75 minutes. Go west on I-66 for almost 21 miles to Exit 43 to get on Hwy 29 South. Stay on Hwy 29 South to Warrenton and follow Hwy 211 West towards Shenandoah National Park and Skyline Drive. Hwy 211 West from Warrenton to Sperryville contains temptations in the form of the Unicorn Winery and Grey Ghost Vineyards - as well as the Inns located in Washington, VA. Stay focused on the ride and return to those spots afterwards! From Sperryville to the Thornton Gap entrance is approximately seven miles with the last four miles being a challenging climb for those wanting to park in Sperryville and earn the right to ride on Skyline Drive! After processing through the entrance station (hopefully by showing your National Parks Pass!), go Left to the Panorama Comfort Station parking lot. Panorama has clean bathrooms and plenty of parking. But DO NOT drink the water! From the Panorama parking lot you can ride North towards Front Royal (a 64 mile roundtrip) or South towards Skyland and further South to the Byrd Visitor Center at Big Meadows (an almost 40 mile roundtrip).

Lay o' the Land

MOUNTAINOUS! Skyline Drive is the original scenic drive in the Blue Ridge Mountains. Rising out of the Shenandoah Valley at Front Royal the initial five miles are all uphill until you get to Dickey Ridge. From there you wind your way along the spine of the Blue Ridge south to Big Meadows. Alternately riding on the western and eastern sides of the ridgetops, as well as down through gaps in the Blue Ridge you see the seemingly endless ridge lines to the west towards West Virginia or look east and see the mountains taper down to the Virginia Piedmont. You will see tall, majestic forests as you ride through the low gaps in the mountains and see the wind-swept, stunted hardwoods along the mountaintops!

Ride Description

Skyline Drive is a 105-mile mountainous road cycling paradise through the beautiful Shenandoah National Park. Skyline Drive has frequent overlooks to rest weary legs and enjoy the views, and has Park stores with restrooms, food and drink. However we focus on the northern half of Skyline Drive from the northern entrance just south of Front Royal to the Byrd Visitor Center at Big Meadows at mile 51. While we consider Skyline Drive to be the best road biking available in northern Virginia, it features challenging riding with steep climbs and equally steep - and fast - descents. An older road, Skyline Drive is relatively narrow with little to no shoulders and sharp - sometimes blind - curves. Though the speed limit is a maximum of 35 MPH, cyclists must exercise caution and ride defensively. Not only are motorists and motorcyclists potential threats but, so are the varied, abundant wildlife living within Shenandoah National Park. Deer are everywhere along Skyline Drive, as are squirrels, turkey and rabbits. Ride Skyline often enough and keep a sharp eye out in the shadows of the forest that edges close to many portions pf the roadway and you are guaranteed to eventually see black bear. We once spotted a juvenile bear creating a bear jam along the roadway as tourist hung out of their vehicle windows with camcorders to film the bear. Less than two miles further we spotted a young cub in the brush about 20 yards off the pavement - there is yet to be an energy

A black bear crossing the road on Skyline Drive during a June, 2010 TNT training ride.

bar made that can provide the adrenaline jolt of realizing you need to put as much distance between yourself and a bear cub as possible! Wherever there is a cub, there is a Momma bear close by!

While you can park and begin your ride at any of the many roadside overlooks we will focus beginning your ride at either the northern entrance to Skyline Drive and the Shenandoah National Park or the Thornton Gap entrance. We also focus on locations where either food or a restroom is available. One of the most appealing things about road biking along Skyline Drive beginning at the northern entrance is you know exactly how far you have ridden just by watching the rock mile markers as you pass them. All you have to do is turn around at a mile marker and ride back to your vehicle. Just double the mileage you rode out and you have your total ride distance. For example if you begin at the northern entrance (Front Royal entrance) and ride to the Elkwallow Wayside store (located at Milepost 24) and return, then you know you've ridden 48 (tough!) miles. The other appealing thing about road biking Skyline Drive is - NO TURNS! You stay on Skyline Drive and either ride south or north and return. Of course there are highway intersections along Skyline Drive, but getting off of Skyline Drive is guaranteed to entail a steep downhill as you exit Skyline Drive and a tough climb to get back onto Skyline Drive so we recommend staying on Skyline Drive.

Carolina Tailwinds van and trailer heading up Skyline Drive at Milepost #1 on its Northern Shenandoah Tour

You can park your car and begin at the northern terminus of Skyline Drive as there are a couple of parking areas on the right side of the road just off Hwy 340 where you can park your vehicle, unload your bike and begin your ride. If you choose to park at this entrance however, we recommend driving up to the Park Entrance and purchase your daily entry fee (good for one week). Then drive back to park and ride. The Rangers will normally just wave you through the entrance as you ride up through the entrance point. One of the benefits of driving up to purchase your daily pass is the Ranger will provide you with an excellent map of Skyline Drive that details the points of interest and facilities found along Skyline Drive. Of course if you purchased an Annual Interagency Pass or obtained an Access Pass as explained in Chapter 1 you can just put your pass in your shirt pocket and ride right through the entrance.

The almost five miles of unrelenting climbing from the Park entrance to the Dickey Ridge Visitor Center is a challenging way to begin any ride and therefore many cyclists drive to Dickey Ridge and begin their rides at that point. Dickey Ridge Visitor Center has terrific views, clean restrooms and cool water - making it both an excellent beginning point for any ride and a good stopping point after the initial, difficult five-mile climb.

After Dickey Ridge Visitor Center, the next point for food or a restroom is at the Elkwallow Wayside (Milepost 24). Elkwallow Wayside has everything a hiker, driver or cyclist needs. Hot sandwiches, cold drinks, picnic tables, souvenirs, gas, restrooms - if you need it, Elkwallow Wayside has it. During the late Spring, throughout the Summer and early fall you will meet hikers hiking the Appalachian Trail - which crosses Skyline Drive numerous times, one of which is at the Elkwallow Wayside. If your ride schedule permits, take the time to talk to the hikers, motorists, and your fellow cyclists who may also be using the Elkwallow Wayside facilities. Maybe you will meet folks like the hiker we once met who told us he hoped to get through Virginia by the end of September. We asked him what was "magic" about the end of September. He told us that was when he got his driver's license back and he thought walking through the woods was a good way to pass the time (the date was August 14)! Elkwallow Wayside has a 24/7 fresh water spigot located on the gas pump side of the building near the ice machine so you can fill your water bottles and keep moving if the Elkwallow Wayside store is closed.

Riding from the Skyline Drive entrance to Elkwallow Wayside and back is a challenging 48-mile ride. The ride south to Elkwallow Wayside is especially challenging. We have found it takes us about two and a half hours (on average) to ride to Elkwallow Wayside but only an hour and a half to return. The final three miles into Elkwallow Wayside are downhill; therefore after a rest stop just long enough for your legs to begin to tighten-up you start your return ride with a three-mile climb. However, the final five-mile downhill from Dickey's Ridge to the Park entrance is a blast! Just ensure you ride safely as it is common to cycle faster than motorists drive!

Continuing the ride south, eight miles after Elkwallow Wayside is the intersection of Hwy 211 and Skyline Drive at Thornton Gap. The Panorama Comfort Station is located just south of the Skyline Drive bridge over Hwy 211. Less than a mile south of Thornton Gap is the only tunnel on Skyline Drive, Marys Rock Tunnel. The tunnel is 600 feet long, and gets just dark enough in the middle that you wish you had a headlight. This tunnel is a slightly uphill ride when traveling south, which adds to the challenge of getting through safely. We recommend conspicuous reflectors on the back of your bike, a headlight and pedaling vigorously to get through the tunnel.

Your next opportunity for food, drink, restrooms and a telephone is at Skyland Resort with entrances at mile 41.7 and 42.5. Skyland Resort also offers lodging and the possibility of an overnight trip by riding from the northern entrance to Skyland Resort - spending the night at a cabin and returning the next day. Skyland Resort is the highest point on Skyline Drive 3,680 feet above sea level. Seven and one half miles further south from Skyland Resort is the Big Meadows Wayside (Milepost 51.2), dining room, cafeteria, gift shop and gas station. Just one mile off of Skyline Drive is the Big Meadows Lodge. In addition to its cabin lodging Big Meadows has camping facilities for the intrepid cyclists. When discussing day-trips from the Washington, D.C. metro area, riding from the northern entrance to Big Meadows and back provides a challenging Century ride (102 miles actually), but also provides numerous stops for food, drink and restroom breaks. Just as riding to Skyland Resort and spending the night is an option, so is riding to Big Meadows however, riding further south along Skyline Drive is probably more than most cyclist care to tackle in a single day.

Alice in her Team in Training jersey @ the Big Meadows directional sign

Shenandoah National Park Facilities in the northern half of Skyline Drive and approximate operating hours. Ask the Ranger at the entry station for the current operating hours:

Dickey Ridge Visitor Center (mile 4.6)
Hours*: ~8:30 a.m. - 5:00 p.m. (May - November)
Restrooms, water, park store

Elkwallow Wayside (mile 24.1)
Hours*: ~9:00 a.m. - 5:30 p.m. (May - November)
Restrooms, water, park store, grill

Skyland Resort (miles 41.7 and 42.5)
Hours*: ~8:30 a.m. - 5:00 p.m.
Restrooms, dining rooms, park store, lodging, Taproom ☺

Big Meadows (mile 51)
Hours*: ~8:00 a.m. - 5:30 p.m.
Restrooms, dining rooms, park store, lodging, Taproom ☺

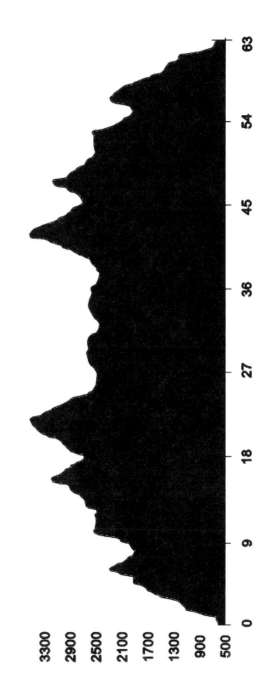

Mile 0 to Thornton Gap & Return Elevation Profile
Start: 596 ft   Low: 596 ft   High: 3,396 ft
Total Gain: 7,744 ft   Distance: 63 mi
Average Elevation Gain: 123 ft/mile

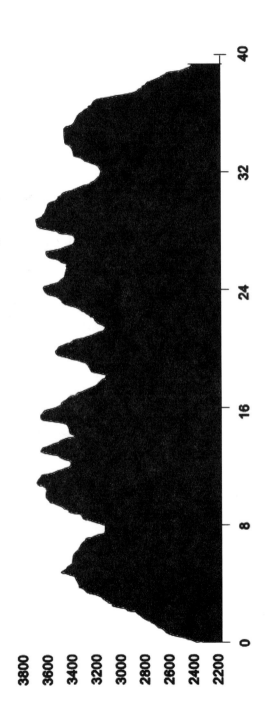

Thornton Gap to Big Meadows & Return Elevation Profile

Start: 2,290 ft   Low: 2,290 ft   High: 3,677 ft

Total Gain: 5,326 ft   Distance: 39 mi

Average Elevation Gain: 137 ft/mile

Mile 0 to Big Meadows & Return Elevation Profile
Start: 596 ft   Low: 596 ft   High: 3,677 ft
Total Gain: 13,070 ft   Distance: 102 mi
Average Elevation Gain: 128 ft/mile

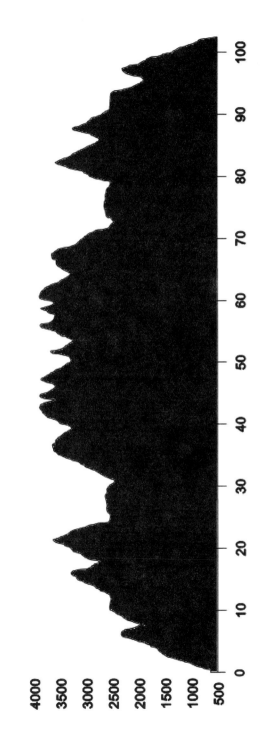

Places to Eat

As we described earlier, Skyline Drive has several places to eat during your ride should you choose to do so. If you begin and end your ride at the northern entrance, then Front Royal has all the regular fast food chains. Our favorite place to eat after riding Skyline Drive is the Jalisco Authentic Mexican Restaurant at 1303 North Royal Ave (Hwy 340 Bus North). The service is friendly and quick, the food plentiful, and the beer cold!

If you begin and end your ride from Thornton Gap and drove Hwy 211 West then you can stop in either Sperryville or Warrenton on your way home. If you begin and end your ride from Thornton Gap and drove Hwy 211 East then you can stop in either Luray or New Market on your way home.

Local Bike Shops

Front Royal does not have any bike shops and there are NO bike shops along Skyline Drive, so you will need to take special care to ensure your bike is prepared for a challenging ride.

If you take Hwy 211 East to Thornton Gap then your best option is to stop in Luray at Hawksbill Bicycles located at 20 West Main St. The phone number and web site are: (540) 743-1037 and www.hawksbillbicycles.com.

Local Attractions

Of course, you are already on one of the most visited attractions in Virginia - Skyline Drive! However, depending upon your selection of starting points there are numerous local attractions that you will be tempted to try to cram into your day's activities. Front Royal is not only a quaint little town with much Civil War history, but it is also the self-proclaimed "Canoe Capital of Virginia." Luray Caverns are only eight miles west in Luray and there are several wineries just off Hwy 211 between Warrenton and Sperryville.

If you complete your ride early and want a cool treat you may want to go tubing on the South Fork of the Shenandoah River. Shenandoah River Outfitters (SRO) - located in Bentonville - is the closest tube rental to either ride ending point. To get there from the northern entrance to Skyline just take Hwy 340 South to Bentonville - about eight miles. Turn Right on SR 613 (Panhandle Rd) for about one mile. SRO is on the left just before the low water bridge. To get there from Thornton Gap take Hwy 211 West for eight miles to Hwy 340 North for 13 miles to Bentonville. Turn Left on SR 613 to get to SRO.

Chester Gap Cellars is one of our favorite wineries. Bernd and Kristi Jung are warm hosts and their wines are awesome! Located, appropriately enough at the Chester Gap in the Blue Ridge mountains, about four miles south of Front Royal on Hwy 522 South (4615 Remount Rd, Front Royal, Virginia 22630). Hours: Fridays 12:00 p.m. - 6 p.m.; Saturdays 11:00 a.m. - 6:00 p.m.; Sundays 12:00 p.m. - 5:00 p.m. Memorial Day and Labor Day 11:00 a.m. - 5:00 p.m. You may also contact Bernd to make an off-hours or private tasting appointment by calling him @ 540-636-8086 or by email @ Bernd@ChesterGapCellars.com

Rappahannock Cellars. Open daily all year 10:30 a.m. - 5:00 p.m. Sat 10:30 a.m. - 6:00 p.m. (540) 635-9398. www.rappahannockcellars.com

Desert Rose Ranch and Winery is an experience! Located at 13726 Hume Rd, Hume, Virginia 22639. House: Thursday-Monday 1:00 p.m. - 6:00 p.m. 540-635-3200. www.desertrosewinery.com

Glen Manor Vineyards makes terrific wines! Jeff focuses on making only quality wines and will not release a wine unless it meets his exacting standards. Address is 2244 Browntown Rd, Front Royal, Virginia 22630. Hours: April-November Wednesday - Saturday 11:00 a.m. - 5:00 p.m., Sundays 12:00 p.m. - 5:00 p.m.; December-March Fridays and Saturdays 11:00 a.m. - 5:00 p.m., Sundays 12:00 p.m. - 5:00 p.m. Closed Thanksgiving Day, Christmas Day through New Year's Day, and Easter Sunday. 540- 635-6324. www.glenmanorvineyards.com

*Bernd Jung, Chester Gap Cellars winemaker, his wife Kristi (center)
and Katie Adzemovic at the tasting bar of Chester Gap Cellars.*

Kevin & Alice enjoying a tasting @ Rappahannock Cellars.

10

Edinburg

How to Get There (where to park)

Getting to the starting point in Edinburg is easy. From the Metro D.C. area take I-66 West to I-81 South to Exit 279. At the bottom of the exit ramp, go Left towards Edinburg. There is a Shell gas station "Bo's Express" on the left. There is plenty of parking at Bo's Express as well as bathrooms, snacks, drinks and fruit (normally bananas are available). Bo's is open 24 hours per day. Coming from Winchester and points north, just take I-81 South to Exit 279. From points south, get on I-81 North to Exit 289. Should the Bo's Express parking lot be full, just continue east towards Edinburg for 1/4 mile to the Shenandoah County Library on the left. The library has plenty of parking and very clean restrooms. The library hours are Monday, Tuesday & Thursday 10:00 a.m. - 8:00 p.m.; Wednesday, Friday 10:00 a.m. - 6:00 p.m.; Saturday 10:00 a.m. - 4:00 p.m. and closed Sunday.

Lay o' the Land

This ride takes you from the low ground along the North Fork of the Shenandoah River in the western portion of the Shenandoah Valley across the valley into the mountains to the west and then back across the valley crossing the North Fork of the Shenandoah River onto the western ramparts of Short Mountain before descending back down to the valley floor. This ride has rolling hills, steep climbs (and descents!), flats alongside rivers and streams, open pastureland, and roads completely covered by overhead forests. You will experience all the beauty the Shenandoah Valley has to offer on this ride!

Route Description

Heading west on SR 675 (Stoney Creek Rd) and Wolf Gap Rd (a Virginia Byway) you climb slightly as you head around the northern tip of Three Mile Mountains and turn southwest onto SR 717 (Liberty Furnace Rd). The first 1.5 miles on Liberty Furnace Rd parallels Big

*Alice takes a water break
after the short climb
to Liberty Furnace*

Stoney Creek before beginning the rolling hills that characterize the remaining 11 miles of SR 717. Pay attention to the turns to stay on SR 717 to stay on the route as the name changes to Alum Springs Rd at approximately mile 12.6! The 263 Diner & Pub is on the right at the intersection of SR 717 and Hwy 263 and makes for a good rest stop.

Three things happen within 3/10th mile on Hwy 263 East. Number 1 - you pass a Community Store on your right which has drinks, snacks and bathrooms. Number 2 - you pass the entrance to Bryce Resort on your left. If you want a longer break, you can take a flat, 3.2 mile loop detour to go to the Bryce Resort Clubhouse for solid food, drinks and clean restrooms. Number 3 - you begin a tough 1-mile climb across Supin Lick Ridge. The beauty is that once you crest Supin Lick Ridge you essentially ride downhill all the way to Hwy 11 in Mount Jackson - almost 10 miles! There is an opportunity for rest stop along Hwy 263 East at the Shenandoah Farm Market on your right at about mile 26.7 (our favorite stop for a scone!). After briefly getting on Hwy 11 through Mt Jackson you cross the North Fork of the Shenandoah River outside of Mt Jackson as you climb onto the western shoulder of Short Mountain and head north to Edinburg. Shortly after re-crossing the North Fork of the Shenandoah River you enter Edinburg and complete this beautiful ride.

The Shenandoah Farm Market has awesome scones!

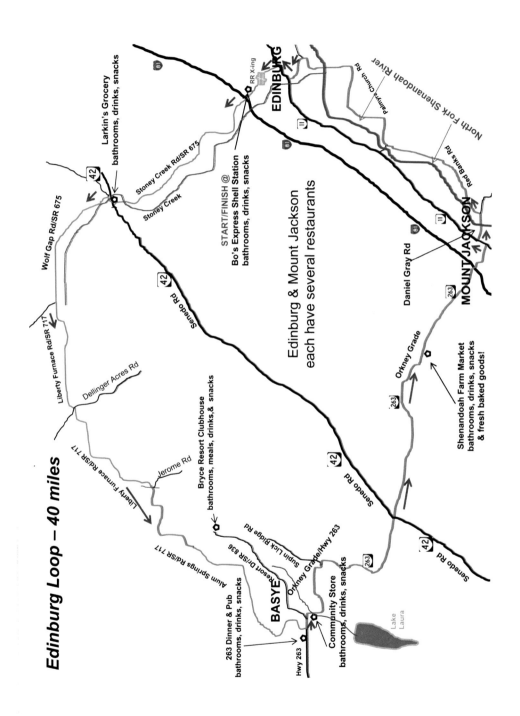

Edinburg Loop – 40 miles

Larkin's Grocery
bathrooms, drinks, snacks

RR X-ing

EDINBURG

North Fork Shenandoah River

Palmyra Church Rd

Red Banks Rd

Stoney Creek Rd/SR 675

Stoney Creek

Wolf Gap Rd/SR 675

START/FINISH @
Bo's Express Shell Station
bathrooms, drinks, snacks

42

42

Senedo Rd

Edinburg & Mount Jackson
each have several restaurants

MOUNT JACKSON

Daniel Gray Rd

263

Liberty Furnace Rd/SR 717

Dellinger Acres Rd

Orkney Grade

Shenandoah Farm Market
bathrooms, drinks, snacks
& fresh baked goods!

263

Liberty Furnace Rd/SR 717

Jerome Rd

Bryce Resort Clubhouse
bathrooms, meals, drinks,& snacks

42

Senedo Rd

Alum Springs Rd/SR 717

Resort Dr/SR 836

Supin Lick Ridge Rd

Orkney Grade/Hwy 263

263

42

Senedo Rd

BASYE

263 Dinner & Pub
bathrooms, drinks, snacks

Hwy 263

Community Store
bathrooms, drinks, snacks

Lake
Laura

~ Refer to page 10 for Ride Map Color Codes ~

Edinburg Loop Cue Sheet

	Total	Segment
R out of **Bo's Express** parking lot onto Stoney Creek Rd (SR 675)		4.8
R @ **SS** on Hwy 42 North; **Larkins Grocery** is on the right corner	4.8	0.1
L on Wolf Gap Rd (SR 675) **VBW**	4.9	3.0
BL on Liberty Furnace Rd (SR 717)	7.9	4.3
BL TRO Liberty Furnace Rd (SR 717)	12.2	0.4
R across bridge to stay on SR 717 (**BEC** Alum Springs Rd)	12.6	1.2
BL TRO Alum Springs Rd (SR 717)	13.8	5.0
L @ **SS** on Hwy 263 East (Orkney Grade Rd)	18.8	10.6
L @ mile 19.0 for optional down & back to **Bryce Resort Clubhouse** (3.2 mile round trip)		
L @ **SS** on Hwy 11 North	29.6	0.2
R on Daniel Gray Dr (SR 698); careful, easy turn to miss!	29.8	3.9
S TRO on SR 698; **BEC** Red Banks Rd	33.7	0.6
BEC Palmyra Church Rd	34.3	1.7
BL TRO Palmyra Church Rd	36.0	0.3
BR TRO Palmyra Church Rd	36.3	0.8
Bridge over North Fork Shenandoah River	37.1	1.3
R @ **SS** on Hwy 11 North	38.4	0.4
L on Stoney Creek Rd (SR 675)	38.8	0.2
2RR	39.0	0.8
R into **Bo's Express** parking lot	39.8	

~ Refer to page 9 for Cue Sheet Symbology ~

Edinburg Loop Elevation Profile
Start: 803 ft   Low: 780 ft   High: 1,679 ft
Total Gain: 3,503 ft   Distance: 40 mi
Average Elevation Gain: 88 ft/mile

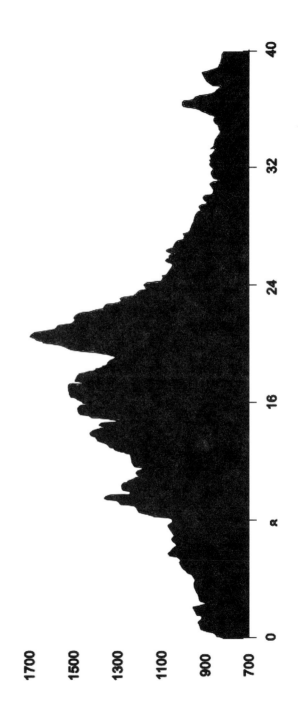

Places to Eat

Edinburg has limited eating places but Sal's Italian Bistro completely makes up for any shortcomings! Sal's is practically a local attraction itself. The quantity of food is exceeded only by its quality. Sal's is a "must eat" location. In addition to Sal's there is a SUBWAY, Larkin's Pizza & Deli, Sweet Sensations and Valley Lunch in Edinburg. If you are returning home to the north then you can go north on Hwy 11 through Woodstock where you will find several chain restaurants as well as some local eateries. If you are returning home to the south, then take Hwy 11 South through Mount Jackson (which has several restaurants) to New Market where you will find Jalisco Authentic Mexican Restaurant #2.

We recommend Sal's!

Local Bike Shops

There are no bike shops along this ride. Ensure your bike is properly tuned before going on this ride and ensure your ride group carries the proper equipment for major roadside repair.

Local Attractions

Like so many of the rides in the Shenandoah Valley, there are enough local attractions to prevent you from riding! We begin with the wineries.

Shenandoah Vineyards has excellent wines and is easily accessible as they are just off the beginning of the route. The hours are March-November 10:00 a.m. - 6:00 p.m. Phone is (540) 984-8699. www.shentel.net/shenvine.

North Mountain Vineyard & Winery is a little farther away but worth the effort - especially if you return to D.C. via I-81 to I-66. Ask John for a "vat tour!" The hours are year round Wednesday-Sunday 11:00 a.m. - 5:00 p.m. Phone is (540) 436-9463. www.northmountainvineyard.com.

Orkney Springs has hosted the Shenandoah Valley Music Festival for the past 44 years and is still going strong. The festival typically runs from mid-July through Labor Day weekend. Just follow Hwy 263 (Orkney Grade) to Orkney Springs! Performances usually begin in late afternoon so you can complete your ride; get changed and make the music festival in the evening. Call (800) 459-3396 for more information or go to www.musicfest.org.

Bryce Resort is a four season resort with something for everyone. Snow Skiing and Tubing in the Winter; Ziplining in the Spring; Golf, fishing, hiking, mountain biking in the Spring, Summer, and Fall - Bryce Resort has it all! There are Chalets available for rent year-round so you could Bryce Resort your base for cycling. Bryceresort.com

Edinburg hosts its own Ole Time Festival the third full weekend in September each year. With plenty of good food, arts, crafts, music and street dances each evening the Ole Time Festival is full of fun times for all!

Alice and Kevin with Emma Randel, owner and driving force behind Shenandoah Vineyards and a pioneer of the Virginia Wine Industry.

Shenandoah Vineyards is the oldest winery in Virginia's Shenandoah Valley.

11

Luray

Alice climbing on Hwy 340 South

How to Get There (Where to Park)

To get to the beautiful ride around Luray you can follow two sets of directions. Here are the directions from the I-66 and I-495 interchange for each route. If you drive via I-66 through Front Royal the drive south on Hwy 340 from Front Royal to Luray is breathtaking with its views of Skyline Drive on the crest of the Blue Ridge Mountains on your left and Massanutten Mountain and the George Washington National Forest on your right. However, the Warrenton-Sperryville drive on Hwy 211 West carries you through portions of northern Virginia's fabulous Wineway and is a more scenic drive than going west on I-66 to Front Royal. We often drive out one way and return the other to take in both sets of scenery!

Luray via I-66 and Hwy 340 South from Front Royal

Go west on I-66 for just over 50 miles to Exit 13. Go Left at the bottom of the exit ramp to the first light where you will go Right on Hwy 55 West. Just as going to Skyline, stay on Hwy 55 West through four lights to the "T" intersection with Hwy 340. Go Left on Hwy 340 South for almost 23 miles where you will enter Luray just after passing under Hwy 211. Turn Right into the Commuter Park and Ride after passing under Hwy 211. The Commuter Park and Ride lot is where we begin our ride around Luray. If you are driving north or south on I-81, take Exit 264 to New Market. From New Market, take Hwy 211 East to Luray. Take a Right on Business Hwy 340 South and another Right into the Commuter Park and Ride lot.

Luray via Hwy 211 through Thornton Gap

Go west on I-66 for almost 21 miles to Exit 43A to get on Hwy 29 South. Stay on Hwy 29 South to Warrenton and follow Hwy 211 West for about 26 miles towards Shenandoah National Park and Skyline Drive. After entering Sperryville, you pass vegetable and fruit stands as well as antique stores on both sides of Hwy 211. From the Thornton Gap intersection with Skyline Drive, it is eight miles on Hwy 211 West to Hwy 340 exit. Go Left at the bottom of the exit ramp onto Hwy 340 South, pass under Hwy 211 and park in the Commuter Park and Ride lot.

Luray from I-81 Corridor

If driving from the I-81 corridor and you are north of the I-66/I-81 interchange, the best way to get to Luray is by taking I-66 East to Exit 6 and then getting Hwy 340 South to Luray. If you are south of the I-66/I-81 interchange then the best way to get to the Luray is to take Exit 264 and get on Hwy 211 East at New Market. Stay on Hwy 211 East for about 16 miles until you come to Luray.

Lay o' The Land

This ride is essentially a circuit of the town of Luray, located in Page County and the entire ride is within the Page Valley section of the northern Shenandoah Valley. The ride is bounded on the west by the Massanutten Mountain and on the east by the Blue Ridge Mountains of the Shenandoah National Park. The first half of the ride features the South Fork of the Shenandoah River while the second half of the ride climbs out of the river lowlands and up onto the lower shoulder of the Blue Ridge Mountains until the final three mile downhill back into Luray. This ride highlights the diversity of agriculture in the Shenandoah Valley. You will pass through bountiful farmland, lush pastures with horses, cattle and goats grazing and several poultry farms. Though characterized by rolling terrain this ride has several climbs that are definitely more than rollers. The roads range from some of the more narrow Scenic Byways to the two-mile section of Hwy 211 - a four-lane highway with wide shoulders and generally low traffic volume.

This ride has some incredible scenery so you will want to have your camera with you as you ride. You cross the South Fork of the

Shenandoah River twice with photo opportunities at each crossing. The first half of the ride features views of Skyline Drive to the east, while the second half of the ride features the Massanutten Mountain to the west with a tremendous view the New Market Gap. During the summer months there is the opportunity to cool off by taking a dip in Lake Arrowhead (approximately mile 28.5 on the ride), the water reservoir for Luray.

Ride Description

This ride almost circles the quaint little town of Luray. Luray is famous for its Luray Caverns - touted as the largest and most popular caverns in the East. No visit to Luray is complete without touring the Caverns so this ride is somewhat short - though certainly challenging! The Commuter Park and Ride has a port-o-john so you can take a final bathroom break before beginning the ride. Riding Right out of the Commuter Park and Ride lot with a quick Right onto Mechanic Street and the challenge begins immediately with an almost 1/2-mile climb to where Mechanic Street crosses Hwy 211 and becomes Bixler's Ferry Road (SR 675). Bixler's Ferry Rd is a winding, rural road with no shoulders so use caution. Once on Bixler's Ferry Rd however you are greeted with views of the northern portion of the Massanutten Mountain as it rises above the Shenandoah River South Fork.

This portion of the ride is rolling pastureland with plenty of cattle in the fields. You will cross over the Shenandoah River South Fork and then turn Left onto North Egypt Bend Rd (still SR 675). Use caution at this intersection as it is a triple yield intersection. This section of North Egypt Bend Rd is a Virginia Byway and you quickly see why with the Shenandoah River South Fork to your left and the Massanutten Mountain rising immediately to your right. About 1/2 mile after getting on North Egypt Bend Rd, you will stay straight on North Egypt Bend Rd, as it becomes (SR 615). Another mile and a half further you will go Right to stay on North Egypt Bend Rd and remain on it for another four miles until you come to the intersection with Hwy 211. On the left at the Stop sign, Outlanders Motorcycles and Customs is open daily and has clean bathrooms, drinks and some food. Turning Right onto Hwy 211 West for the next two miles, you will want to stay on the right shoulder of this four-lane highway with grass median. Though not heavily traveled, it is a high-speed road but by staying to the right, you will give motorists plenty of room to safely pass on your left.

Turn Left onto Hwy 340 South where you will find yourself on a one-mile gradual climb on an excellent road with wide shoulders (our book cover photo!). You pass the Page Valley Flea Market on the left (open weekends year round) about one mile before taking a Left onto

Kevin w/Bear @ Outlanders -
Massanutten Mountain in background

Hwy 340 North Business. After crossing the Shenandoah River South Fork, the Riverside Mini Mart and Deli with its assortment of food and drink - and bathrooms is on the right! Continue on Hwy 340 North Business through the small town of Stanley (Main Street in Stanley). Stanley has several food establishments and bathroom possibilities. Use caution crossing the slightly angled, raised railroad tracks at mile 19.7. Take a Right on Chapel Rd (SR 689) to exit Stanley. Chapel Rd becomes Marksville Rd after about 1/2 mile. Stay to the Left on Marksville Rd before the bridge over Hawksbill Creek. After going Left onto Ida Rd (still SR 689) you are treated to a beautiful view of Massanutten Mountain and the New Market Gap on your left and the Shenandoah National Park and Skyline Drive on your right. Stay on Ida Rd for four miles before taking a Right on Valley Burg Rd (SR 668).

Approximately a mile later, stay straight on Valley Burg Rd. Take a Right onto Lake Arrowhead Rd (SR 669) at the Stop sign and you can take the Left into Lake Arrowhead Park 0.2 mile further. Lake Arrowhead has "outhouse" style bathrooms and several picnic shelters long with a sand beach and swimming from Memorial Day to Labor Day. The beach has a canteen, which sells drinks in season. Lake Arrowhead also has some Nature Trails if you would like to take a break from the bike. After getting back on Lake Arrowhead Rd (exit Left out of Lake Arrowhead Park) the road narrows and has some loose gravel on it to the next turn onto Dry Run Rd so use caution. Go Left on Dry Run Rd (SR 667) and enjoy almost four miles of uninterrupted gradual downhill - you will have earned it! At the Stop sign on Hwy 211 West Business, take a Left to downtown Luray being careful at the angled railroad crossing at mile 35.3. Just down the hill from the rail-road-crossing, take a Right at the light onto Hwy 340 North Business (Broad St) for less than 1/2 mile back to the Commuter Park and Ride on the left.

Luray Loop – 36 miles

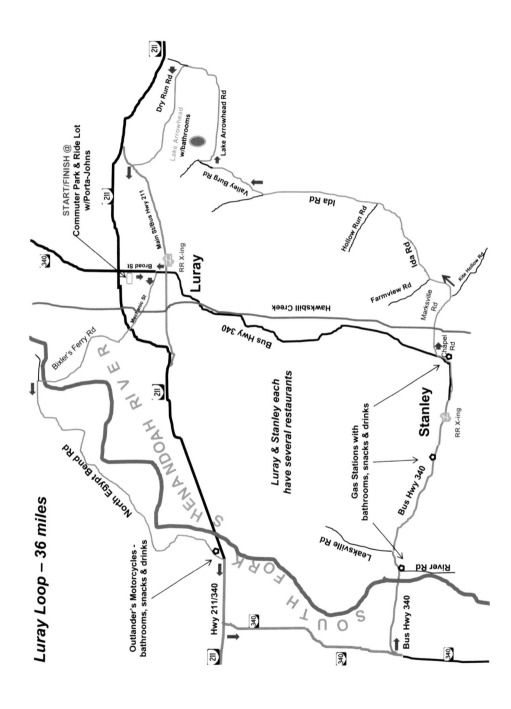

Luray Loop Cue Sheet

	Total	Segment
R out of Commuter Park & Ride onto Hwy 340 South Business (North Broad St)		0.2
R on Mechanic St	0.2	0.8
Cross Hwy 211; **BEC** Bixler's Ferry Rd (SR 675)	1.0	2.6
L on North Egypt Bend Rd (SR 675) after bridge over the South Fork of the Shenandoah River	3.6	0.4
S on North Egypt Bend Rd (**BEC** SR 615)	4.0	1.5
R TRO North Egypt Bend Rd	5.5	4.1
R on Hwy 211 West; **Outlanders** on corner	9.6	1.9
L on Hwy 340 South	11.5	3.1
L on Hwy 340 North Business	14.6	3.9
Enter Stanley	18.5	1.2
RR (RAISED/ANGLED)	19.7	0.4
R on Chapel Rd (SR 689)	20.1	0.4
BEC Marksville Rd (SR 689)	20.5	0.4
BL before bridge over Hawksbill Creek	20.9	1.0
L on Ida Rd (SR 668)	21.9	4.0
R on Valley Burg Rd (SR 668)	25.9	0.9
S on Valley Burg Rd (SR 668)	26.8	1.5
R on Lake Arrowhead Rd (SR 669)	28.3	1.6
Lake Arrowhead Park on left @ mile 28.5		
L on Dry Run Rd (SR 667)	29.9	3.8
L on Hwy 211 West Business (East Main St)	33.7	1.6
RR (ANGLED)	35.3	0.1
R @ **TL** on Hwy 340 North Business (North Broad St)	35.4	0.5
L into Commuter Park & Ride Parking Lot	35.6	

~ Refer to page 9 for Cue Sheet Symbology ~

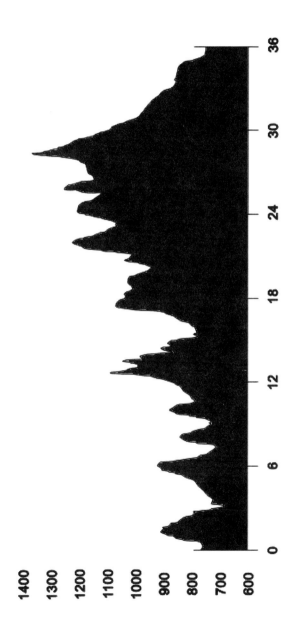

Luray Loop Elevation Profile

Start: 760 ft   Low: 693 ft   High: 1,390 ft

Total Gain: 3,255 ft   Distance: 36 mi

Average Elevation Gain: 90 ft/mile

Places to Eat

There are plenty of places to grab drinks and snacks or eat a meal along the route but Luray has a wide assortment of eating establishments for such a small town. There are local eateries such as Mrs. B's Pizza, the Southern Station Diner, The Lunch Box, Uncle Buck's Restaurant and Lounge. Additionally there is an Expresso Café, the Artisans Grill and the Woodruff Inn's Victorian Inn. Crossing Hwy 340 onto West Main Street there is the West Main Street Market - known for serving fresh foods, and The Mimslyn Inn that features a buffet lunch on Sundays.

Local Bike Shop

Hawksbill Bicycles located at 20 West Main St is Luray's only bike shop. Owner Chris Gould is active in every aspect of cycling in Page County and helps coordinate and sponsor several events each year. Stop by to see them! The phone number and web site are: (540) 743-1037 and www.hawksbillbicycles.com.

Hawksbill Bicycles has everything you need!

Local Attractions

The main attractions in Luray are the world famous **Luray Caverns**. Open year-round the caverns are spectacular and well worth visiting after your ride. The guided tour takes an hour and tours leave approximately every 20 minutes beginning at 9:00 a.m. Closing times vary with the season between 4:00 p.m. and 7:00 p.m. Remember the inside temperature of the cave is approximately 65 degrees so you may want to bring a light jacket to wear on the tour. The caverns have clean bathrooms, a café, a Garden Maze and a Car and Carriage Caravan Museum. The phone number and web site are: (540) 743-6551 and www.LurayCaverns.com.

This ride takes you by **Wisteria Farm and Vineyard** after passing through Stanley. Open March through Christmas with $5 tastings. Hours are Monday 12:00 p.m. - 6:00 p.m.; Tuesday & Wednesday no hours are specified; Thursday through Sunday 12:00 p.m. to 6:00 p.m. The phone number and web site are: (540) 742-1489 and www.wisteriavineyard.com.

The other attraction you may wish to visit is **Skyline Drive**. The closest entry point onto Skyline Drive is via Thornton Gap located eight miles east of Luray on Hwy 211 East. Skyline Drive is beautiful whether you are bicycling or driving. From Thornton Gap to the northern entrance at Front Royal is 32 miles - make sure you stop at the overlooks for some awesome views!

12

New Market

How to Get There (where to park)

Getting to New Market, VA and the Hall of Valor Museum parking lot is simple. Take I-66 West to I-81 South to Exit 264 (New Market exit). At the bottom of the exit ramp go Right & take an immediate Right (almost a right-handed U-turn) onto the George R. Collins Memorial Highway. Drive approximately one mile through the gate to the Hall of Valor Museum parking lot. There is plentiful parking at the Museum as well as picnic tables, clean bathrooms and vending machines offering snacks, soft drinks, juices and bottled water. There is also a water fountain. The museum is open from 9 a.m. - 5 p.m. daily. Not only does the museum close at 5 p.m. but the gate also closes! Speaking from experience you CAN be locked into the parking lot. Ensure you give yourself enough time to complete the rides before 5 p.m.!

In addition to the Hall of Valor parking there is the New Market Community Park, which is open from dawn to dusk. Better yet - there is no gate to the Community Park so you do not have to watch your time so closely. However, the Community Park only has seasonal

Kevin checking air pressure in Hall of Valor parking lot. Restrooms and Welcome Center in the background.

bathrooms and no vending machines. To get to the Community Park, you take a Left at the bottom of the Exit 264 ramp; then go Right at the first light (0.2 mi) on Cadet Rd and stay on Cadet Rd to the New Market Community Park. The Community Park is 0.8 mile from the exit off I-81. The Community Park has a seasonal pool, picnic tables and even a fitness trail for those needing even more exercise after their ride!

If coming north from the Winchester area or south from Staunton or Lexington, just get on I-81 to Exit 264 and follow the directions above.

Lay o' the Land

These three rides are located predominantly within Shenandoah County but do cross south into Rockingham County. It is character-ized by gorgeous rolling, typically open farm and pastureland. You will ride past cattle and crops as well as poultry farms. These rides fea-ture several crossings of the North Fork of the Shenandoah River as well as passing through the quaint towns of Mt. Jackson, Timberville, and Broadway. There are too many photo opportunities to mention so carry a camera with you! There are also many places to take breaks and relax.

Ride Descriptions

We have three rides we enjoy which begin in New Market. The first two are each just over 36 miles (just under if departing from the Community Park) while the third ride is essentially a combination of the first two rides. The first we call the Broadway Loop and the sec-ond we call the Meems Bottom Covered Bridge ride. Each ride takes you through spectacular scenery of the northern portion of the Shenandoah Valley however; we think the Meems Bottom Covered Bridge ride is the more challenging ride of the two. The third ride we call New Market Loop and since it is a combination of the first two we only provide a map and a cue sheet for that ride rather than another detailed description.

Broadway Loop Description

Exiting the Hall of Valor parking lot follow the George R. Collins Memorial Highway to the Right back to Hwy 211 West. Go Right on Hwy 211 West for over five virtually flat miles to the intersection with Hwy 42. There is an Exxon station with deli and bathrooms on the left corner in case you forgot any food or drink for this relatively short, easy ride. There are some food locations on the left just after the turn

- possibly for post-ride pizza! Stay on Hwy 42 South for a less than two miles and then take a Right onto Hwy 259 West towards Broadway. The first of two railroad crossings on the Broadway Loop occurs at mile 8.4 followed less than a 1/2 mile later by a 24-hour Shell station with Sub and Deli shop on the right. This portion of the ride is especially nice as you parallel the Shenandoah River North Fork until turning onto North Mountain Rd (SR 613). North Mountain Rd is a smaller rural road that begins with a 1.5 mile gradual climb followed by winding slight climbs and descents along its entirety. There are spectacular views to both sides as you travel on North Mountain Rd for almost nine miles before coming to the Stop sign where you take a Right back onto Hwy 42 South - Senedo Rd. Just over a mile after getting back on Hwy 42 South, you pass Paugh's Orchard on the right where you can get seasonal fresh fruit.

Alice takes a gel break on Hwy 42 South

In Forestville, take a Right at the Stop sign to stay on Hwy 42 South (do not miss the chance for cold drinks at the This or That Country Store on the right immediately after the turn!). You have a scenic five miles before entering Timberville. As you enter Timberville, you will have a long downhill that requires caution - especially as your next turn sneaks up on you! About the time you hit maximum speed on the downhill you will pass a Dodge dealership on the right and need to slow down, as your Left hand turn onto Church Street (SR 617) is only about 200 meters past the Dodge dealership and less than 100 meters before a railroad crossing. As the turn immediately becomes a short steep climb, you will want to be in your climbing gear before making the turn. Improper gearing will ensure you are "dancing on the pedals" as you climb this steep hill! Following the climb up Church St, you then have a longer, slightly less steep downhill through a residential neighborhood before the road flows onto a long flat after making 90-degree Right turn; crossing railroad tracks and an immediate 90-degree Left turn. Be careful - safely cross the tracks before starting your turn. You now have a three-mile flat section where you can see the New Market gap on the horizon ahead of you off to your "1 o'clock" position. Evergreen Valley Rd carries you back across the Shenandoah River North Fork to Hwy 211 where you go Left back towards I-81 and then Left back onto the George R. Collins Memorial Highway to the Hall of Valor museum parking lot.

Meems Bottom Covered Bridge Ride Description

Exit the Hall of Valor parking lot on the George R. Collins Memorial Highway to Hwy 211 West just as on the Broadway Loop ride. Go Right on Hwy 211 West for 0.7 mile and go Right on Plains Mill Rd (SR 953). Immediately after crossing the bridge over the Shenandoah River North Fork, take a Right on River Rd (SR 617). Stay straight on

Canadian friends Linda Vaz
& Mira Svodoba exit
Meems Bottom Covered Bridge

River Road at the sharp turn. This section is flat as it parallels the river before turning sharply away from the river. There is a railroad crossing at 3.6 miles as you begin a climb. There is a Yield sign at about 5.3 miles where you stay straight though the name changes to Ridge Rd (SR 616). In Quicksburg, go Left on Ridge Rd (SR 616) and then Left onto Quicksburg Rd (SR 767) at the Stop sign after about 50 meters. Quicksburg Rd is winding until you turn Right on Turkey Knob Rd (SR 698).

If you are looking to take a detour to see Shenandoah Caves or America on Parade, you can take a Right at mile 8 and follow the signs. Both attractions are within one mile of the turn and have bathrooms available. Continue on Turkey Knob Rd until taking a Right on Wissler Rd (SR 720) where you cross some railroad tracks. At just over nine miles, you cross over I-81. Just prior to crossing I-81 you can take a Right onto SR 950 (Industrial Park) for about 1/4-mile to the Route 11 Potato Chip Factory. The factory tour does not take long and the chips are terrific! After crossing I-81, make your way down some sharp turns to Meems Bottom Covered Bridge at 9.5 miles. Meems Bottom Covered Bridge is a one-lane bridge nestled into a shaded nook of the Shenandoah River North Fork. It is always a cool spot - even in the heat of summer - and makes for a terrific photo opportunity. Just be

Kevin detouring to
Shenandoah Caverns

careful of cars coming in either direction and of the wooden flooring of the bridge. It is easy to catch a front wheel in the dim light and possibly fall. After a 1/2-mile, take a Left at the Stop sign onto Hwy 11 North towards Mt Jackson. Hwy 11 narrows on the bridge across the Shenandoah River North Fork. Turn Left onto Hwy 263 (Orkney Grade Rd) - a Virginia Byway - in Mt Jackson. Should you need a bathroom break you can continue on Hwy 11 into Mt Jackson where you will find the Mt Jackson Visitor's Center, which is open afternoons and Saturdays from 10 a.m. - 4 p.m. Further into Mt Jackson, you will find a Liberty gas station on the right with bathrooms and 1.2 miles from the turn on Hwy 263, you will find several fast food restaurants. Hwy 263 is named Orkney Grade Rd because it rises gradually up to cross Supin Lick Mountain before descending towards Orkney Springs - home of the annual Shenandoah Valley Music Festival - and to Bryce Resort. However, our route keeps you on Hwy 263 for just over six miles before turning onto Hwy 42 South (Senedo Rd).

Fresh bread at the Shenandoah Farm Market

We would be remiss if we did not mention the Shenandoah Farm Market on the left about halfway to Hwy 42. They have drinks, snacks and fresh baked goods (pie, cookies, and bread) and are a great stop for a treat! After turning Left on Hwy 42 South, you immediately cross a bridge over Mill Creek and then a Trout Farm on your left before beginning a gradual climb.

At Getz Corner at mile 20 take a Right on North Mountain Rd (SR 613). You get to see the same beautiful scenery as you did on the Broadway Loop ride - just now in the opposite direction! Stay on North Mountain Rd for just five miles and take a Left on Orchard Drive (SR 881). Orchard Drive takes you to Timberville where you will take a Right at the Stop sign back onto Hwy 42 South. Less than 1/4 mile after turning onto Hwy 42 South you come a railroad crossing with a Chevron station (with bathrooms) on the left immediately after the railroad crossing and immediately before yet another bridge across the Shenandoah River North Fork. About 1/2 mile after the bridge, take a Left onto Hwy 211 East towards New Market. If you have ridden the Broadway Loop ride first, then this section will be familiar as it is the initial portion of the Broadway Loop ride. While it makes a great warm-up for the Broadway Loop ride, this almost six mile flat back into New Market makes for either a great cool down or final push for speed to complete the ride. Stay on Hwy 211 East until taking a Left (just before I-81) onto the George R. Collins Memorial Highway back to the Hall of Valor Museum parking lot.

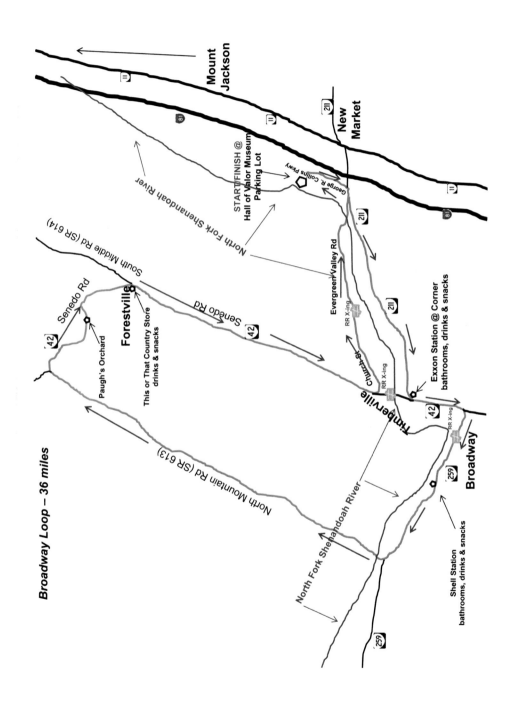

Broadway Loop Cue Sheet

	Total	Segment
R out of **Hall of Valor Museum** parking lot on the George R. Collins Parkway		1.0
R on Hwy 211 West (Lee Hwy)	1.0	5.5
L @ **TL** on Hwy 42 South; **Exxon** on corner	6.5	1.3
R on Hwy 259 (Brocks Gap Rd)	7.8	0.6
RR	8.4	3.4
R on North Mountain Rd (SR 613)	11.8	8.7
R @ **SS** on Hwy 42 South (Senedo Rd)	20.5	3.4
R @ **SS TRO** Hwy 42 South (Senedo Rd)	23.9	5.9
L on Church St (SR 617); **STEEP CLIMB**; **BEC** Evergreen Valley Rd	29.8	1.2
RR (CAUTION - sharp turn immediately after crossing tracks	31.0	3.4
L @ **SS** on Hwy 211 East	34.4	0.8
L on George R. Collins Parkway	35.2	1.0
L into **Hall of Valor Museum** parking lot	36.2	

~ Refer to page 9 for Cue Sheet Symbology ~

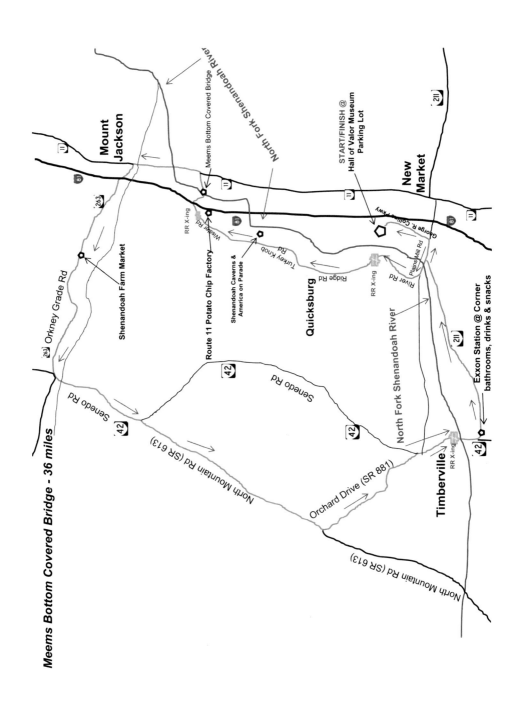

Meems Bottom Covered Bridge - 36 miles

~ *Refer to page 10 for Ride Map Color Codes* ~

Meems Bottom Covered Bridge Cue Sheet

	Total	Segment
R out of **Hall of Valor Museum** parking lot on the George R. Collins Parkway		1.0
R on Hwy 211 West (Lee Hwy)	1.0	0.7
R on Plains Mill Rd (SR 953)	1.7	0.5
R on River Rd (SR 617); then **S**	2.2	1.4
RR	3.6	1.7
S @ **YS BEC** Ridge Rd (SR 616)	5.3	0.6
L on Ridge Rd (SR 616); **L** after 50 yds on Quicksburg Rd (SR 767)	5.9	0.8
R on Turkey Knob Rd (SR 698)	6.7	1.9
R on Wissler Rd (SR 720)	8.6	0.2
RR	8.8	0.7
Detour to **Route 11 Potato Chip Factory** before bridge over I-81		
Meems Bottom Covered Bridge	9.5	0.5
L on Hwy 11 North	10.0	1.6
L on Hwy 263 West (Orkney Grade Rd)	11.6	6.1
L on Hwy 42 South (Senedo Rd)	17.7	2.3
R on North Mountain Rd (SR 613)	20.0	5.3
L on Orchard Dr (SR 881)	25.3	3.8
R on Hwy 42 South	29.1	0.2
RR (**Chevron** station w/bathroom on left)	29.3	0.5
L @ **TL** on Hwy 211 East (New Market Rd)	29.8	5.4
L on the George R. Collins Parkway	35.2	1.0
L into **Hall of Valor Museum** parking lot	36.2	

~ Refer to page 9 for Cue Sheet Symbology ~

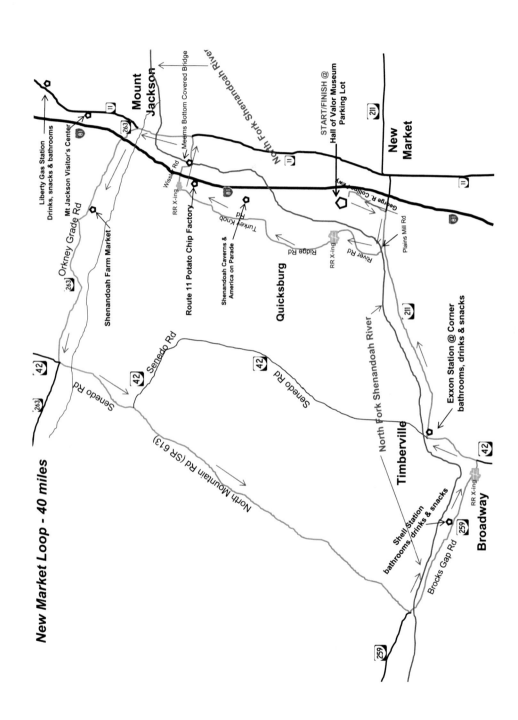

New Market Loop - 40 miles

~ Refer to page 10 for Ride Map Color Codes ~

New Market Loop Cue Sheet

	Total	Segment
R out of **Hall of Valor Museum** parking lot on the George R. Collins Parkway		1.0
R on Hwy 211 West (Lee Hwy)	1.0	0.7
R on Plains Mill Rd (SR 953)	1.7	0.5
R on after bridge River Rd (SR 617); then **S**	2.2	1.4
RR	3.6	1.7
S @ **YS BEC** Ridge Rd (SR 616)	5.3	0.6
L on Ridge Rd (SR 616); **L** after 50 yds on Quicksburg Rd (SR 767)	5.9	0.8
R on Turkey Knob Rd (SR 698)	6.7	1.9
R on Wissler Rd (SR 720)	8.6	0.2
RR	8.8	0.7
Detour to **Route 11 Potato Chip Factory** before bridge over I-81		
Meems Bottom Covered Bridge	9.5	0.5
L on Hwy 11 North	10.0	1.6
L on Hwy 263 West (Orkney Grade Rd)	11.6	6.1
L on Hwy 42 South (Senedo Rd)	17.7	2.3
R on North Mountain Rd (SR 613)	20.0	8.7
L @ **SS** on Brocks Gap Rd	28.7	3.5
RR	32.2	0.5
L @ **SS** on Hwy 42 North	32.7	1.3
R @ **TL** on Hwy 211 East (New Market Rd); **Exxon** w/bathroom on corner	34.0	5.4
L on the George R. Collins Parkway	39.4	1.0
L into **Hall of Valor Museum** parking lot	40.4	

~ Refer to page 9 for Cue Sheet Symbology ~

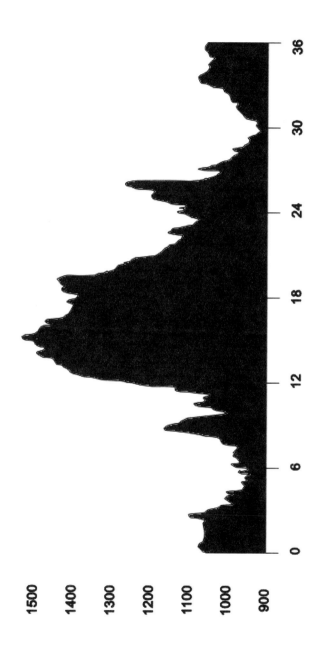

Broadway Loop Elevation Profile
Start: 1,060 ft   Low: 932 ft   High: 1,502 ft
Total Gain: 2,463 ft   Distance: 36 mi
Average Elevation Gain: 68 ft/mile

Meems Bottom Covered Bridge Elevation Profile
Start: 1,060 ft   Low: 860 ft   High: 1,502 ft
Total Gain: 2,299 ft   Distance: 36 mi
Average Elevation Gain: 64 ft/mile

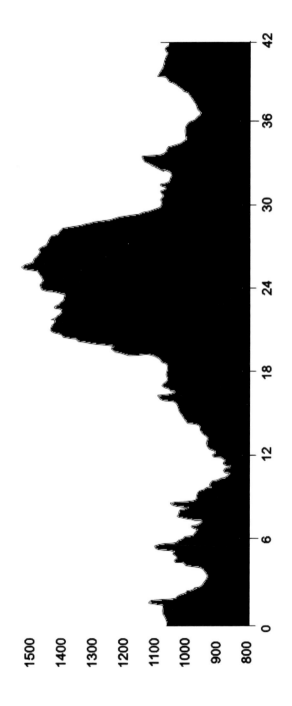

New Market Loop Elevation Profile
Start: 1,060 ft   Low: 860 ft   High: 1,502 ft
Total Gain: 3,066 ft   Distance: 41 mi
Average Elevation Gain: 75 ft/mile

Places to Eat

New Market has a surprising variety of places to carb up after your ride - from fast food to full service restaurants. Everything is conveniently located either just off the I-81 exit ramp or along New Market's Main Street (Highway 11). Our favorite post-ride eatery is Jalisco Authentic Mexican Restaurant #2 located on Main Street. Jalisco's has a unique slaw served with their chips that we think is incredibly good. They also serve standard salsa and - importantly - cold beers! Jalisco's prices are low but the serving portions are large so this is a great deal after a ride!

Local Bike Shops

There are no bike shops in New Market or along any of the routes. Ensure your bike is properly tuned before going on this ride and ensure the ride group carries the proper equipment for major roadside repair.

Local Attractions

New Market has enough local attractions to keep you busy without going for a bike ride! The best known - and closest - is the **New Market Battlefield** and **Hall of Valor Museum**. On May 15, 1864, teenage Cadets from the Virginia Military Institute fought in the battle. That battle is re-enacted each year in mid-May, on the grounds of the Hall of Valor Civil War Museum in New Market. The Battlefield is open daily 9:00 a.m. - 5:00 p.m. except for Thanksgiving, Christmas Eve, Christmas Day and New Year's Day. Other attractions include:

Shenandoah Caverns and American Celebration on Parade are located just off the Broadway Loop route - take a break from pedaling and see them! They are both open daily except for Christmas Day. www.shenandoahcaverns.com

Route 11 Potato Chips Factory is located at 11 Edwards Way, Mount Jackson, Virginia 22842. Open Monday-Saturday from 9:00 a.m. - 5:00 p.m. The cooking schedule varies so call ahead if you make sure you see them cooking their awesome chips - 1-800-294-SPUD. www.rt11.com

Shenandoah Vineyards is just north off I-81. Open daily except for Thanksgiving, Christmas and New Year's. www.shentel.net/shenvine/.

Alice in Route 11 Potato Chip Factory

Endless Caverns is three miles south of New Market just off Highway 11. Endless Caverns is open daily except for Thanksgiving, Christmas and New Year's. www.endlesscaverns.com

13

Harrisonburg

The corner of South Main and East Water streets is located in the heart of downtown Harrisonburg's Renaissance Shopping & Dining District.

How to Get There (where to park)

Harrisonburg is the second farthest drive from the D.C. metro area but the ride around Harrisonburg is well worth the effort. The drive to Harrisonburg is just under two hours from the I-66 and I-495 (D.C. Beltway) intersection. Leaving D.C., take I-66 West to I-81 South to Exit 243. Take the exit to Hwy 11 and take Hwy 11 South for one mile where you will find the entrance to the Shenandoah Heritage Market on the left. The large parking lot is open daily and the Market itself is open every day except Sunday. Harrisonburg is over an hour drive south on I-81 from Winchester and about an hour from Charlottesville via I-64 West and then I-81 North.

Lay o' The Land

Harrisonburg is situated about 10 miles west of the Massanutten peak (and the Massanutten Resort) in the center of Rockingham

County, and offers a variety of cycling possibilities. It is easy to get outside of the built-up area of town and into the rolling countryside so characteristic of the Shenandoah Valley. The ride around Harrisonburg goes through farms and pastureland with some spectacular old farm houses! Rockingham County was settled by the Mennonites and you may find yourself behind a typical black, horse-drawn buggy on any of the roadways. The pungent odor of working cattle farms is a constant companion during this 44+ mile ride. You also ride around one of two extinct volcanoes in Virginia - Mole Hill!

Ride Description

The Shenandoah Heritage Market
has food, drinks, and clean bathrooms!

Take a Right out of the Shenandoah Heritage Market parking lot onto Hwy 11 North for 0.2 mile and take a Left onto Pike Church Road. You experience a 1/2-mile climb that rewards you with terrific views to the south and southwest across the valley floor and looking towards the rolling ridges of the Appalachians. Pike Church Road takes you to a crossing of Hwy 42 in the town of Dayton. Should you have forgotten to stock-up with food and rink, Dayton provides an opportunity for snacks and drinks at the Mini-Market on Main Street. Exiting Dayton you also pass within 0.2 mile of Mole Hill Bikes (go straight at the Stop Sign instead of Left onto SR 732. Mole Hill Bikes is 0.2 mile down the road on the right). Silver Lake Road takes you past, yep, Silver Lake on the left before taking a series of roads circling Mole Hill before getting onto Hwy 33 East. Stop to take a good look at Mole Hill as you

Mole Hill has the distinctive cone shape of a volcano!

circle and you can see the cone of the extinct volcano! Getting on Cooks Creek Rd off of Hwy 33 takes you north to Singers Glen Road through pasturelands and working farms.

At Singers Glen Road you turn Right (east) back towards Harrisonburg. Singers Glen runs into and becomes Mount Clinton Pike with a 0.6 mile climb to Eastern Mennonite University on your left. Cross Hwy 42 and continue until you come to Hwy 11. Be careful crossing the quadruple railroad crossing at mile 11.3! Turn Left on Hwy 11 North for 0.8 mile and take a Right onto SR 720 (Smithland Rd). Be careful as the turn onto SR 720 is easy to miss. Go Left at the Stop sign on SR 718 and cross over I-81. Once you cross I-81 you quickly get onto SR 717 - Indian Trail Rd that you follow for four miles of rolling roads northward before cutting across Fridley's Gap Road to Mountain Valley Road. Upon turning Right (south) on Mountain Valley Road, you immediately notice the Massanutten Mountain on your left. Mountain Valley Road is a winding, hilly and slightly uphill ride for 10 miles. In the pastures closely lining the roadway you will see cows, llamas, horses, mules, donkeys, goats and possibly pigs! Additionally you will pass both large working farming operations and abandoned farmhouses.

As you cross Hwy 33 the ride flattens slightly until you turn Right (west) onto Pleasant Valley Road. Pleasant Valley Road has a climb for about a mile until you come to the 3-way Stop. You are then rewarded for the slight rest by another rolling climb of almost one mile. However, there's a terrific view towards the southwest as you crest the hill and begin about a mile of downhill until turning Left onto Cecil Wampler (SR 704). Cecil Wampler takes you back across I-81 to Hwy 11 where you turn Right on Hwy 11 North for one mile and turn into the Shenandoah Heritage Market on the right.

Alice passing bales of hay on Smithland Rd

Al Williams, Bob Marsh, and Carol Gardner relax by the pool after a day on the bike during Bike Virginia 2011

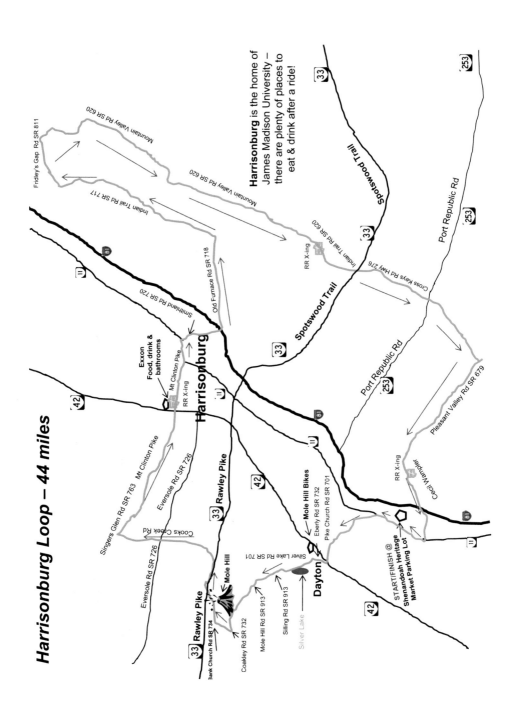

Harrisonburg Loop – 44 miles

Harrisonburg is the home of James Madison University – there are plenty of places to eat & drink after a ride!

Fridley's Gap Rd SR 811

Mountain Valley Rd SR 620

Mountain Valley Rd SR 620

Indian Trail Rd SR 717

Indian Trail Rd SR 620

Old Furnace Rd SR 718

Smithland Rd SR 720

Exxon
Food, drink &
bathrooms

Mt Clinton Pike

RR X-ing

Harrisonburg

Mt Clinton Pike

Singers Glen Rd SR 763

Eversole Rd SR 726

Cooks Creek Rd

Eversole Rd SR 726

Rawley Pike

33 Rawley Pike

Bank Church Rd SR 734

Coakley Rd SR 732

Mole Hill

Mole Hill Rd SR 913

Silling Rd SR 913

Silver Lake Rd SR 701

Dayton

Silver Lake

Mole Hill Bikes

Eberly Rd SR 732

Pike Church Rd SR 701

START/FINISH @
Shenandoah Heritage
Market Parking Lot

Cecil Wampler

RR X-ing

Pleasant Valley Rd SR 679

Port Republic Rd

Port Republic Rd

Cross Keys Rd Hwy 276

RR X-ing

Indian Trail Rd SR 620

Spotswood Trail

Spotswood Trail

33

33

33

42

42

42

11

11

11

253

253

253

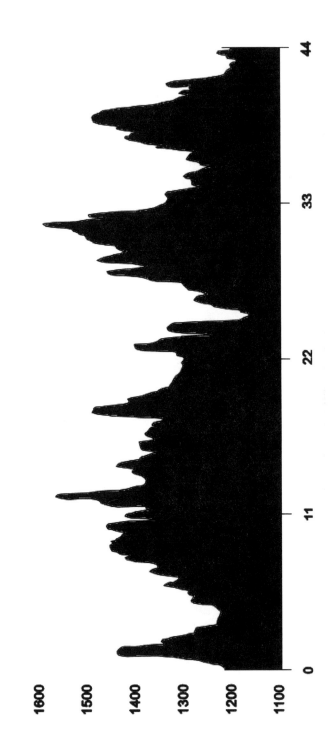

Harrisonburg Loop Elevation Profile
Start: 1,210 ft   Low: 1,151 ft   High: 1,561 ft
Total Gain: 5,012 ft   Distance: 44 mi
Average Elevation Gain: 114 ft/mile

Harrisonburg Loop Cue Sheet

	Total	Segment
R out of **Shenandoah Heritage Market** parking lot on Hwy 11 North		0.2
L on Pike Church Rd to SR 701	0.2	1.4
L @ **SS TRO** SR 701 (West Mosby Rd)	1.6	0.5
SA Hwy 42 @ **TL**	2.1	0.1
R @ **SS** on Hwy 42 North Business (Main St)	2.2	0.4
L @ **SS** on Eberly Rd (SR 732)	2.6	0.3
R @ **SS** on Silver Lake Rd (SR 701)	2.9	0.6
Silver Lake on left @ mile 3.1		
L on Silling Rd (SR 913)	3.5	0.4
R on Swope Rd (SR 736)	3.9	0.2
L on Mole Hill Rd (SR 913)	4.1	1.0
Mole Hill (extinct volcano) on right	5.1	0.5
R on Coakley Town Rd (SR 732)	5.6	0.1
R TRO Coakley Town Rd (SR 732)	5.7	0.3
R on Bank Church Rd (SR 734)	6.0	1.1
R on Hwy 33 East (Rawley Pike); **CAUTION** - cars crest hill from the left quickly!	7.1	1.0
L on Cooks Creek Rd (SR 701)	8.1	1.4
SA SR 725 @ **SS**; **CAUTION** - cars crest hill from the left quickly! Just after the church on the left stay straight **TRO** Cooks Creek Rd	9.5	1.0
Sharp R @ **SS** on Singers Glen Rd (SR 763)	10.5	3.3
SA Hwy 42 @ **TL** - **Exxon** on corner	13.8	0.1
4RR	13.9	0.4

(continued on back)

~ Refer to page 9 for Cue Sheet Symbology ~

	Total	Segment
SA Liberty St @ **TL**	14.3	0.8
L @ **TL** on Hwy 11 North	15.1	0.7
R on Smithland Rd (SR 720) - easy to miss!	15.8	0.8
L @ **SS** to SR 718 - cross over I-81	16.6	0.2
BEC Old Furnace Rd (SR 718)	16.8	2.3
L @ **SS** on Indian Trail Rd (SR 717) - **SS** @ bottom of hill	19.1	0.6
BL TRO Indian Trail Rd (SR 717)	19.7	3.7
BR TRO Indian Trail Rd (SR 717)	23.4	0.3
R on Fridleys Gap Rd (SR 811) easy to miss!	23.7	2.5
R on Mountain Valley Rd (SR 620)	26.2	2.6
BL TRO Mountain Valley Rd (SR 620)	28.8	0.5
BL TRO Mountain Valley Rd (SR 620)	29.3	4.0
L @ **SS TRO** SR 620; **BEC** Indian Trail Rd - careful of the angled **RR** 100 yards after the turn	33.3	1.6
SA Hwy 33 @ **TL**; **BEC** Hwy 276 (Cross Keys Rd)	34.9	2.1
SA Hwy 253 @ **TL**	37.0	1.0
R on Pleasant Valley Rd (SR 679) - hilly uphill!	38.0	0.9
S @ **3WS**	38.9	2.5
L on Cecil Wampler Rd (SR 704)	41.4	0.3
2RR	41.7	0.5
L @ **SS TRO** Cecil Wampler Rd (SR 704)	42.2	1.3
R @ **SS** on Hwy 11 North	43.5	1.0
R into **Shenandoah Heritage Market** parking lot	44.5	

Places to Eat

Should you decide not to take advantage of the terrific home cooked buffet at the Shenandoah Heritage Market, Harrisonburg is a typical college town with all of the expected fast food and pizza locations. However, James Madison University has a strong alumni base and Parent Council with many alums returning for athletic and artistic events so Harrisonburg also has many nice restaurants where you can replenish your carbohydrates stores. Harrisonburg has a selection and price to fit every palate and budget with many nationally known chain restaurants along Hwy 33 East of I-81.

Local Bike Shops

Harrisonburg has two excellent bike shops in town and another, Mole Hill Bikes is located just down the road (and just off the route) in Dayton. Here are the addresses, phone numbers and business hours of the bike shops, all easily accessible while on the Harrisonburg ride.

Shenandoah Bicycle Company, located in downtown Harrisonburg is a spacious, full service bicycle shop - complete with an Acai smoothie bar!

Shenandoah Bicycle Company located at 135 South Main St, Harrisonburg, VA 22801 is open 11:00 a.m. - 7:00 p.m. Monday - Friday; 9:00 a.m. - 4:00 p.m. Saturday. Phone: (540) 437-9000. www.shenandoahbicycle.com

Mark's Bike Shop located at 1570 South Main St, Harrisonburg, VA 22801 is open 10:00 a.m. - 7:00 p.m. Monday - Friday; 10:00 a.m. - 4:00 p.m. Saturday. Phone: (540) 434-5151.

Mole Hill Bikes located at 440 North Main St, Dayton, VA 22821 is open 10:00 a.m. - 6:00 p.m. Monday - Friday; 10:00 a.m. - 5:00 p.m. Saturday. Phone: (540) 879-2011.

Wrenching at Mole Hill Bikes

Local Attractions

Harrisonburg is home to **James Madison University**. 15 miles east of Harrisonburg is the Massanutten Resort - a four season resort. Snow skiing and golf are the two big attractions at the resort but they also have swimming pools, fitness center, hiking dining and accommodations.

Between Bridgewater and Harrisonburg are two terrific markets featuring just about anything you would care to find! The **Shenandoah Heritage Market** (where we recommend you begin this ride) is located between Dayton and Harrisonburg just off Hwy 11 North. The Shenandoah Heritage Market features fresh vegetables, home cooked buffet, antiques, quilts, homemade jams and jellies and bookstore practically dedicated to the Civil War history of the Shenandoah Valley. The Shenandoah Heritage Market has something for everyone so plan on spending some time there before or after your ride.

The **Dayton Farmers Market** is located on Hwy 42 South in Dayton. Open year round Thursday-Saturday from 9:00 a.m. - 6:00 p.m. the Dayton Farmers Market has over 20 locally owned shops with a restaurant on-site. The website is www.daytonfarmersmarket.com. The phone number is (540) 879-3801.

14

Bridgewater

How to Get There (where to park)

Amish buggies can be a familiar sight on both rides from Bridgewater

In addition to being the farthest drive from the D.C. metro area the Bridgewater rides are also two of the most challenging rides in our book. The Reddish Knob ride has 10 continuous miles of uphill and downhill! The Todd Lake ride has almost 10 miles of continuous downhill riding as well! Though the drive is roughly two hours from the I-66 and I-495 (D.C. Beltway) intersection, it is easy to get there. Leaving D.C., take I-66 West to I-81 South to Exit 240 - the Bridgewater College exit. Follow Hwy 257 West from the exit for approximately two and a half miles to the entrance to Bridgewater College. Immediately prior to the Bridgewater College entrance, turn Left onto College View Drive. Go to the Stop sign and turn Right onto East College View for a short distance before turning into the Visitors, Faculty and Staff parking lot. Do not park in the Faculty and Staff section of the parking area! Both rides begin and end in the Visitors, Faculty and Staff parking area. The good news for Charlottesville area cyclists is these are the closest rides to Charlottesville! Just take I-64 West to I-81 and then go north to Exit 240 and follow the directions above.

Lay o' the Land

The Reddish Knob ride has tremendous variety of terrain and displays everything of beauty you can expect from the Shenandoah Valley. There are stretches of gently rolling terrain through fertile farmland and dairy farms as well as upland hardwood forests characteristic of the Appalachian Mountains. There is a 10+-mile climb from the valley floor to the top of Reddish Knob - elevation of 4,397 feet! Reddish Knob is the highest point in northern VA and straddles the VA-WV border. From the top of Reddish Knob, you can see from the New Market Gap to the southern end of the Massanutten Mountain and even further south. Bridgewater is located within a portion of the Shenandoah Valley settled by Mennonites and you may find yourself passing the black buggies pulled by horses (watch out for droppings!) along any of the rolling roads before and after the climb to Reddish Knob. You also need to watch out for cattle droppings on the road as fresh cow piles are especially slick.

The Todd Lake ride also has tremendous variety of terrain. However rather than the highest point in northern Virginia, the destination point is a scenic mountain lake with swimming area and a sandy beach!

Ride Descriptions

Reddish Knob

Kevin after conquering the climb to Reddish Knob

The Reddish Knob ride begins quietly through the Bridgewater College campus along East College View before going through the old downtown portion of Bridgewater on South Main St and then crossing the North River. There is then about eight miles of cleared rolling farm and pastureland before beginning the climb to Reddish Knob at mile nine. On the right side of the road at the Left turn onto Hwy 257 West is the 257 Grocery. Nice folks run the 257 Grocery store, which has a grill, snacks, drinks and clean bathrooms.

The ride changes character rather dramatically as you enter the George Washington National Forest and the climb to Reddish Knob. Almost imperceptibly at the 9-mile mark, the climbing begins and does not become noticeable until entering the George Washington National Forest (at mile 10.3). When the road becomes SR 924, you will notice several things occurring simultaneously. First the condition of the roadway itself deteriorates; there are potholes and gravel in the roadway through the remainder of the climb. Second, the roadway becomes almost completely covered by the limbs of the trees on both sides of the road. Third is the now noticeable incline that will stay with you all the way to Reddish Knob itself, except for a three-tenths of a mile portion just before Reddish Knob. You will pass Hone Quarry Lake and dam on the left at about the 14-mile point. There are primitive bathrooms available at the dam. The views from Reddish Knob are worth the effort to get there! 360-degrees of beauty! Reddish Knob is tabletop flat and makes a terrific picnic spot if you have a SAG vehicle to bring up food and drink. It tends to be windy on top so a windbreaker is a good item to have - even in summer!

Clearly, the return ride from Reddish Knob begins with 10 miles of downhill with the first six miles the most challenging. Use the utmost caution coming down as the road is narrow; the turns sharp; and the potholes in the road have been filled with asphalt with a gravel top. Listen for cars coming UP the hill so you are not surprised in the middle of a turn. The loose gravel, potholes and crumbled road edges are more problematic on the way down as you are traveling faster with much more momentum than on your way up. However, having mentioned all of the precautions - the ride down is a BLAST! Do not be surprised if you pass cars on the way down - you will smell their brakes as you go past. Once past the dam the road becomes less steep and by the time you exit the George Washington National Forest the downhill is barely noticeable all the way back to the 257 Grocery.

The final 10+ miles after coming down the hill from Reddish Knob and turning left onto Hwy 257 East are back to rolling hills (OK, a couple of the hills are bigger than rollers) through beautiful Shenandoah Valley pastureland. You will pass big farmhouses, big barns and silos on both sides of the road on the ride back to Bridgewater College. Continue to watch the road for animal droppings as the farmers move their cattle from pasture to pasture along the roads and the animals sometimes seem to delight in soiling the road! We once saw a llama, goat, pigs with piglets, a bull and an ostrich all in the same pasture - a great photo op!

Todd Lake

The Todd Lake ride features many of the same features as the Reddish Knob ride - just different! You will ride though much more pastureland on the Todd Lake ride. The views to the West along Centerville Rd from 1.5 mi - 4.2 mi are stunning as you essentially climb along a ridge to SR 646. Roman Rd gives new meaning to backcountry road! The narrow road is about as rural as you can get in Virginia and as the "NO

Amanda & Alice at the Todd Lake beach

SERVICE" on your cell phone will attest. Be careful on SR 607, as it is one of those country roads with loose gravel covering the paved surface. Catching a patch of gravel in a turn is not a good idea so use caution and go slow on the downhills. A timely point to take a break is at Dorsey's Market on the right at mile 18.4. Dorsey's has snacks, drinks and most importantly - clean bathrooms! Rolling roads through pastures describe the route until begin climbing on SR 718 to Todd Lake. Most of the ride along SR 718 is completely covered by trees with the additional cooling factor that the road rises along Skidmore Fork as it tumbles to the North River.

Alice & Kevin take a break on the bridge across the North River enroute to Todd Lake

You can really feel the cooling effects of the shade and creek even though you are mostly climbing to Todd Lake. Todd Lake is a small mountain lake featuring a sandy beach, bathrooms, changing rooms, picnic tables and a shower. In fact, if you only wanted to ride 30 miles, Todd Lake makes a terrific place for a picnic lunch after a ride! There is an entry fee for cars but those who purchased a National Parks annual pass pay 1/2 the regular entry fee.

The ride down from Todd Lake is terrific. It is not as steep as the descent from Reddish Knob but is almost as long since the ride essentially continues slightly downhill paralleling the North River for several miles all the way to the turn onto SR 727. At about mile 39 you can take a Right across the North River onto Natural Chimney Rd for an optional trip to Natural Chimneys Regional Park and Campground. Natural Chimneys has a camp store where you can purchase cold drinks and snacks. Back on the main route, you turn Right to stay on SR 727 at mile 43.6 and then you return along the same 4.1 miles of the beginning of the Reddish Knob ride.

Though EVERYONE should ALWAYS wear a helmet, Bridgewater requires helmets for all riders age 14 and younger. Bridgewater also prohibits the use of earphones or IPODs while biking.

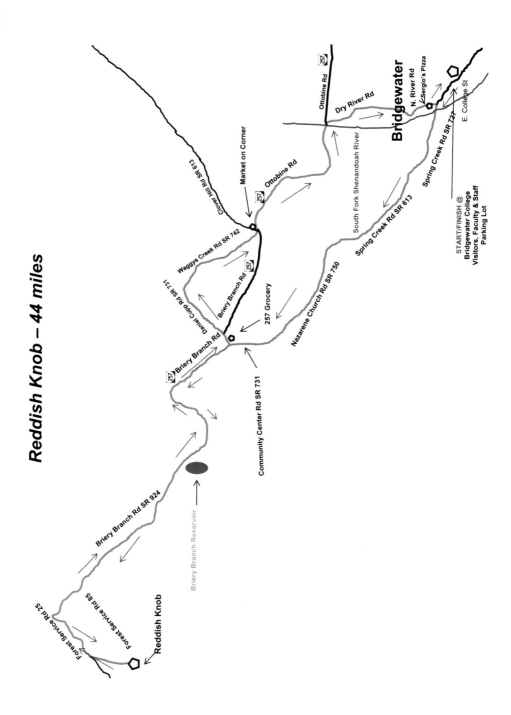

Reddish Knob – 44 miles

Bridgewater

START/FINISH @
Bridgewater College
Visitors, Faculty & Staff
Parking Lot

Sergio's Pizza

N. River Rd

E. College St

Spring Creek Rd SR 727

Dry River Rd

Ottobine Rd

South Fork Shenandoah River

Spring Creek Rd SR 613

Nazarene Church Rd SR 750

257 Grocery

Market on Corner

Ottobine Rd

Colony Hill Rd SR 613

Waggys Creek Rd SR 742

Daniel Cupp Rd SR 731

Briery Branch Rd

Briery Branch Rd

Community Center Rd SR 731

Briery Branch Reservoir

Briery Branch Rd SR 924

Forest Service Rd 85

Forest Service Rd 25

Reddish Knob

~ Refer to page 10 for Ride Map Color Codes ~

Reddish Knob Cue Sheet

	Total	Segment
R out of parking lot on East College St		0.5
L @ **TL** on South Main St	0.5	0.4
R on Spring Creek Rd (SR 727) after bridge	0.9	3.2
R @ **SS TRO** Spring Creek Rd (SR 613)	4.1	0.7
L on Nazarene Church Rd (SR 750)	4.8	3.2
R @ **SS** on Community Center Rd (SR 731)	8.0	0.9
L on Briery Branch Rd (Hwy 257 West)	8.9	4.9
S TRO Briery Branch Rd (SR 924)	13.8	4.5
U-turn to left to stay on paved roadway	18.3	2.3
Reddish Knob!	20.6	2.3
U-turn to right to stay on paved roadway	22.9	9.2
L @ **SS** on Hwy 257 East	32.2	0.2
L on Daniel Cupp Rd (SR 731)	32.4	1.5
R @ **SS** on Waggys Creek Rd (SR 742)	33.9	1.5
S @ **SS** on Hwy 257 East (Ottobine Rd)	35.4	2.2
R on Silver Creek Rd (SR 752); **BEC** SR 909	37.6	1.3
BEC Thomas Spring Rd (SR 748)	38.9	0.4
R @ **SS** on Hwy 257 East (Ottobine Rd)	39.3	0.7
R on Dry River Rd after crossing bridge	40.0	2.5
L @ **SS** on North River Rd	42.5	0.2
R @ **SS** on Main St	42.7	0.5
L @ 2nd **TL** on East College St	43.3	0.5
L into parking lot	43.8	

~ Refer to page 9 for Cue Sheet Symbology ~

Todd Lake – 48 miles

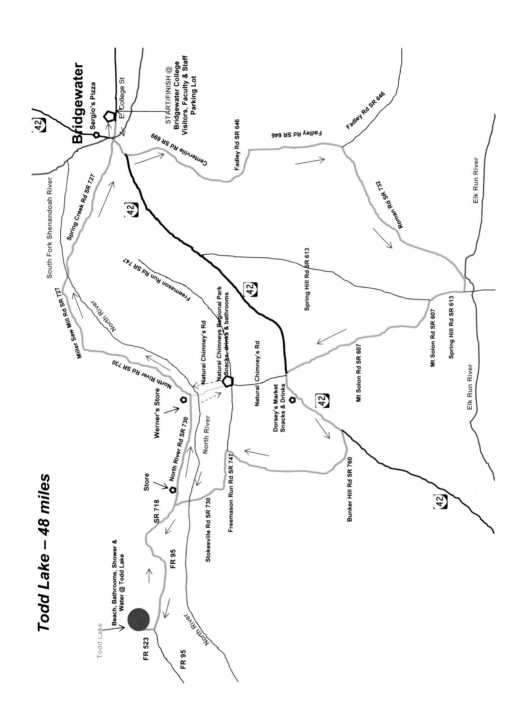

Todd Lake Cue Sheet

	Total	Segment
R out of parking lot on East College St		0.5
L @ **TL** on South Main St	0.5	0.9
L on Centerville Rd (SR 699)	1.4	2.8
L @ **SS** on Fadley Rd (SR 646)	4.2	3.1
S on Roman Rd (SR 732)	7.3	5.3
R @ **SS** on Spring Hill Rd (SR 613)	12.6	1.0
BL on Mt Solon Rd (SR 607)	13.6	4.3
L @ **SS** on Hwy 42 South	17.9	2.7
R on Bunker Hill Rd (SR 760)	20.6	3.4
L @ **SS** on Freemason Run Rd (SR 747)	24.0	1.0
S on Stokesville Rd (SR 73)	25.0	1.0
BL TRO Stokesville Rd (SR 730)	26.0	0.3
S TRO Stokesville RD (SR 718)	26.3	1.0
BL on Fire Rd (FR) 95	27.3	3.1
R on FR 523 to **Todd Lake** parking area	30.4	0.4
Todd Lake parking area	30.8	0.5
L @ **SS** on FR 95	31.3	4.0
L on North River Rd (SR 730)	35.3	5.9
R @ Mile 38.9 on Natural Chimney Rd for 0.3 miles to Natural Chimneys Regional Park. Werner's Store on left @ the turn		
R on Millers Saw Mill Rd (SR 727); store on right	41.2	2.4
BR TRO SR 727; **BEC** Spring Creek Rd	43.6	3.3
L @ **SS** on Hwy 42 North	46.9	0.3
R @ **TL** on East College St	47.2	0.6
L into parking lot	47.8	

~ *Refer to page 9 for Cue Sheet Symbology* ~

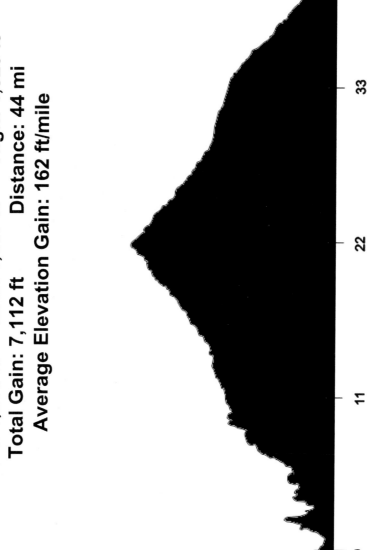

Reddish Knob Elevation Profile

Start: 1,200 ft   Low: 1,167 ft   High: 4,329 ft

Total Gain: 7,112 ft   Distance: 44 mi

Average Elevation Gain: 162 ft/mile

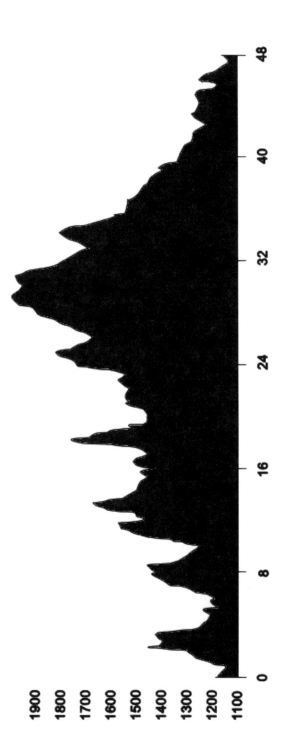

Todd Lake Elevation Profile

Start: 1,190 ft   Low: 1,168 ft   High: 1,948 ft
Total Gain: 4,292 ft   Distance: 48 mi
Average Elevation Gain: 89 ft/mile

Places to Eat

Bridgewater College is a small college - so you will find several typical collegiate restaurants. An excellent local pizza joint is Sergio's Pizza, which you will pass on Main St about a mile from the end of the Reddish Knob ride. They serve terrific made-to-order pizza and ice-cold beer! There is a Quarles gas station on the right serving subs, sandwiches and drinks before turning left onto East College St. The North River Grill is located at the intersection of East College St and Main St and the Red Apple Chinese Buffet on is South Main St.

Sergio's Pizza & Subs is our favorite post-ride eatery in Bridgewater!

Local Bike Shops

There are no bike shops in Bridgewater. The closest is **Mole Hill Bikes** at 440 North Main St, in Dayton - about three miles north of Bridgewater just off Hwy 42. The Mole Hill Bikes is open 10:00 a.m. - 6:00 p.m. Monday-Friday; 10:00 a.m. - 5:00 p.m. Saturday; and closed Sunday. Phone: (540) 879-2011.

Local Attractions

Bridgewater is located off the beaten path - the local attractions are the beautiful countryside and some of its quaint shops. Both Reddish Knob and Todd Lake are terrific attractions themselves. Each is a great location for a picnic. In fact, starting and ending your Todd Lake ride at the lake parking lot is a favorite of some cyclists. Not far southwest of Bridgewater is **Natural Chimneys** - a formation left over from when the entire Shenandoah Valley was covered by an inland sea. Getting to Natural Chimneys is easy - requiring only a 3/10th mile detour from the route. Natural Chimneys hosts events year-round and makes for a fun and educational visit. Natural Chimneys does not charge an entry fee for cyclist. The Natural Chimneys web-site is www.naturalchimneys.com. Check it out for seasonal events

Alice, Lilly, Kevin, Pierre & Amanda
at the base of one of the Natural Chimneys

such as the jousting tournaments in June - normally father's day weekend - and August for the Natural Chimneys Joust - the USA's longest running continuously held sporting event!

The **Shenandoah Heritage Market** and the **Dayton Farmers Market** - both described in Chapter 11 are also easily accessible if you choose to ride either of the Bridgewater rides. Just take Hwy 11 North to the Shenandoah Heritage Market on your right or take Hwy 42 North to the Dayton Farmers Market on your left.

The Dayton Farmers Market is always an enjoyable stop.

Afterward

We learn to road bike by getting out and riding - getting yourself out on your bike for the first ride may be the most difficult thing you do in road biking in northern Virginia. We hope you will feel the same sense of accomplishment we did as you expand your rides beyond those we have listed in this book and enjoy exploring the beautiful, historic northern Virginia and northern Shenandoah Valley.

The first step is getting out and exploring, the next step - riding - is up to you. We hope you will take that step. Refer to this book as you ride. Make notes in it. Tell us your experiences. Let us know where this book can be improved. When you do complete that first ride (or several rides), please send us a note telling us of your experiences. Give us your permission and we may publish your vignette in a future revision. Best of luck!

On your left!

Kevin Watson
Alice Muellerweiss

Selected Virginia Cycling Clubs

Washington Area Bicyclist Association
(202) 518-0524
www.waba.org

Winchester Wheelmen, Inc.
www.winchesterwheelmen.org

Charlottesville Bicycle Club
www.cvillebikeclub.org

Warrenton Cycling
(540) 341-7702
www.warrentoncycling.com

The Reston Bike Club (RBC)
www.restonbikeclub.org

Potomac Pedalers Touring Club (PPTC)
www.bikepptc.org

Babes on Bikes
www.babesonbikes.org

Shenandoah Valley Bicycle Coalition
www.svbcoalition.org

Blue Ridge Bicycle Club
www.brbcva.org